Basketball's
Man/Zone Defense

Basketball's
Man/Zone Defense

Bob Fuller

PARKER PUBLISHING COMPANY, INC.
West Nyack, N.Y.

© 1978 by
Parker Publishing Company, Inc.

West Nyack, N.Y.

Library of Congress Cataloging in Publication Data

Fuller, Bob,
  Basketball's man/zone defense.

  Includes index.
  1. Basketball--Defense. 2. Basketball coaching.
I. Title.
GV888.F84   796.32'32   77-24743
ISBN 0-13-072355-X

Printed in the United States of America

To my present and former players who have so willingly sacrificed individual accomplishments for all-out team efforts, young men dedicated, as only their coach knows, to rank almost annually among the state's top defensive teams

To Virgil E. Little, who gave me my first basketball position and who has forgotten more basketball than I will ever know. Coach Little retired with a lifetime record of 365–179 in 1967

To my top two assistant coaches and cheerleaders, wife Cheryl and daughter Wendy

I dedicate this book.

Also by the Author

Basketball's Wishbone Offense

FOREWORD

The facts and figures speak loudly when basketball talk turns to Bob Fuller. In this case, numbers don't disguise the truth.

A head coach at the high school level in Indiana and Illinois for the past 15 years, Fuller has shunned centering his basketball programs around high-powered offenses and instead concentrated upon developing one of the prep rank's dazzling defenses. Scoring points, enough to avoid a defeat, against a Bob Fuller-coached unit has become a wearisome task.

Utilizing the varying concepts of this book's topic—Basketball's Man/Zone Defense—Fuller has seen his teams achieve impressive goals. Consider the following:

In four years at Highland High School in Anderson, Indiana, Fuller has fashioned a 78–13 record. His 1976 team was ranked second in the state, finished the regular season at 20–0, went on to capture the school's first-ever Sectional and Regional tournament championships and topped Hoosierland with a 46.4 defensive average. For his career Bob has an almost unbelievable record of 318–74.

Prior to Fuller's arrival, Highland had managed only a 34% win mark in 18 years with only one trophy in the showcase; in four years under Fuller the Scots have won 4 conference and 7 tourneys or city titles.

In 12 of 15 years under Fuller's direction, teams have held

opponents to a yearly defensive average of less than 50 points per game. They've limited offenses to less than 50 points in 192 of 392 contests including games of 8, 17, 19, 22, 24, 25, 27 and 29 points.

Such defensive displays have enabled Fuller to run up his amazing record, including 20 tournament and 13 conference championships. His slate stands at 220–41 in 10 years with Hoosier schools and that winning percentage—a lofty .843—ranks No. 1 among active coaches in Indiana. The likable and sometimes controversial coach has never suffered a losing season.

The basis for Fuller's basketball successes are outlined in this book as he explains the tested and proven Man/Zone defensive setup and its derivatives which have been responsible for numerous upsets over high-scoring opponents.

Such results are difficult to argue with.

Mike Chappell

Sports Editor
Anderson Daily Bulletin
Anderson, Indiana

WHAT THE
MAN/ZONE DEFENSE
WILL DO FOR YOU

The most important factor in building a basketball team of championship calibre is to develop a hustling, aggressive team defense. We stress defense because it can be counted on game in and game out, whereas an offense may run hot and cold. A weak defense invites runner-up finishes.

A majority of high school and college coaches have a defensive basketball philosophy. They believe that a zone type of defense has a place in strategy, but do not regard it as their primary defense. Man-to-man defense is the only way they say. I have attended clinics and other coaching get-togethers and have heard many coaches state that "a zone-type team cannot win a major championship or a top-flight tournament." Statements such as these have always come as a direct challenge to me.

I belong to the minority group believing that a zone-type defense is best, especially for the coach who works with average talent year in and year out. This method of coaching has been highly successful for us. Our play is a little unorthodox on both defense and offense so as to make our opponents play a little differently.

The main portions of this book will be the tested and proven

Man/Zone defense and its derivatives which have forced many upset victories over high scoring offensive teams. The most points ever scored against the Man/Zone defense in regulation play is 75 over a fifteen-year period!

This book introduces a unique defense. While structurally a zone-type defense, it incorporates the strong features of both zone and man-to-man defenses, thus the name Man/Zone. During 85% of my coaching career, I've been "blessed" to work with small players of average talent and the Man/Zone defense has been a vital factor in defeating many bigger and stronger squads. Recently I coached two tall, but slow ball clubs and the Man/Zone met with equal success.

The various pressure and trapping Man/Zone defenses that have proven devastating to opponents are described in detail, along with fundamental drills to bring you more victories. Also in this book are our Ten Defensive Commandments that will improve your defensive play. Our special rebounding techniques and drills, alternating defenses, special tactical situations, and practice gimmicks and charts are all structured to give you that extra "winning edge."

All the theories and principles used in our defensive system are described as clearly and simply as possible. I believe that this effort will be of value to open-minded coaches who are in search of championship ideas. We have achieved this goal by following the techniques described in this book.

As you read the succeeding chapters, keep in mind the following statement: *Coaches and teams build reputations with high powered offensive systems, but they* **win** *games with a good defense.*

Bob Fuller

CONTENTS

Basketball's
Man/Zone Defense

1

DEVELOPING THE
MAN/ZONE DEFENSE

THE ORIGIN OF THE MAN/ZONE

The Man/Zone defense has been highly instrumental in our team's 80% win record, including 20 tournament championships and 13 conference titles in 15 seasons. While offense has been a major factor in our success, we strongly feel defense has been the "deciding" measure. We work many hours on defense and tell our players that "we are best because we work harder." Our players feel they can go on the floor against anybody and be in the game.

My philosophy of defense began to form when I was a player on an A.A.U. team. We were entered in a National Tournament in Buffalo, New York and had three players who averaged over 20 points per game each while the team itself carried slightly over 92 per game. We rolled over our first four opponents in the 32-team affair, maintaining our 90-plus offensive average while "holding" the opposition to a 70-plus average. In the championship game we were stifled by our opponent's defense and/or our inability to hit the basket for a decent percentage. We managed a meager 57 points while our defense remained constant in allowing 74 points. After this game my philosophy of defense was formulated. Whether it was the sticky defense of our opponents that had been the deciding factor or our own ineptness to score, it was obvious that offense can be a great variable.

There is never an excuse for an "off night" on defense. On offense you may have your star guard shoot ten jumpshots from 21 feet one night and make eight. The next evening he may go 2 for 10 from the same range. Offense is variable, but defense should be constant. Any offensive team can have a bad game. There are also a frightening number of ways an offensive team can turn the ball over without getting a good shot, such as cupping the ball, traveling, a bad pass, charging foul, double dribble, 10-second violation, 3-second violation, etc. A strong defensive team is always a dangerous opponent. A poor defense places a great hardship on the offense. A team with a strong defense *knows* it can remain in any game.

We used the Man/Zone in our first year of coaching and still use the same principles today with great success at the high school, A.A.U., and independent recreational levels. We do not use the Man/Zone at the lower levels (any level lower than varsity) because we require the strict use of man-to-man defense at these levels, since man-to-man fundamentals are vital to the success of the Man/Zone. We may on occasion play some form of man-to-man defense, but 99% of the time we stick to the Man/Zone or one of its derivatives. Our theory is that it is better to teach one type of defense (Man/ Zone) well than to teach several in a haphazard manner.

When a player has an adequate man-to-man background, we can teach him the Man/Zone basics in the three or four week pre-season preparation time. We have also gotten the Man/Zone ready for action in small periods of time. Once we taught it in a 4-day, one hour per day practice time when coaching in an all-star game. This defense was instrumental in our two game sweep of this series.

We have heard sports fans and coaches say you have to score

points to please the spectators. I totally disagree with these state-ments because the average fan wants to see a winner. I have seen many empty gyms with high scoring but losing ball clubs.

We have shut teams out for an entire quarter on 16 separate occasions and have held teams to scores of less than 30 points in an entire game ten times. We *do not stall* the ball on offense. Some teams establish a fine defensive reputation because they use a slow-down or stalling offense. In 15 years of coaching we have used a straight slowdown offense the entire game only twice. In both cases we felt we were totally outclassed in ability.

More often than not the reason for the low scores comes from the fact that our opponents have trouble penetrating our defense. For example, we have a film of a conference championship game with a high scoring (over 75 points per game), fast breaking opponent. Our team averaged slightly over three passes per possession of the ball while our opponents used over seventeen passes per possession! We won the game 47–37, but the low score was obviously due to the inability of our opponents to attack the Man/Zone.

We try to convince our players that while everybody cannot be a prolific scorer, everyone can learn to play defense. We will take the fast break, but will not spend a lot of time on the outlet pass or other principles of the fast break.

Any player capable of walking on the basketball court can be taught to play defense and play it well. We don't believe in the old saying that a good offense is the best defense. A good offense is a good offense and a good defense is a good defense. When two equally good offensive teams battle, the loser is the one with defects in its defense.

When you give a group of boys a basketball and say "go out on the floor and play," they are going to go out and start shooting but are not going to go out and play defense. Instilling a pride in defense isn't easy because it is something that does not come naturally. Many textbooks on basketball by the great coaches state that ideally you should have a 60% offense/40% defense practice ratio in rela-tion to time. We stress exactly the opposite. I have often pondered that a coach should find the five best defensive players and teach them to play offense!

POSSESSION SCORING PERCENTAGE FORMULA

Defensive averages or the average number of points allowed against a team is not necessarily a true and valid criterion for measuring team defensive ability. Many teams use a slowdown or stalling type of offense that will naturally keep the score down. While this may be excellent strategy, the low score is the result of the offense and should not be credited to the defense.

The number of points allowed is not the *best* indicator of the kind of defense you play. We base the strength of our defense on:

1. Points per Possession
    We use the Possession Scoring Percentage Formula which will be explained in detail later in this section. We shoot for a .75 PSP and try to hold the opponents under a .60 PSP.

2. Field Goal Percentage of opponents
    We strive to hold the opposition under 40% from the field. On a yearly average the opponents have never averaged over 40%, the highest being 39.3%. The opponents have a 15-year average of 37.4%.

3. Rebound Ratio
    We strive for a 10 to 8 rebound ratio. Despite the fact that we are at a definite height disadvantage in a majority of our games, in 15 seasons we have been out-rebounded in only two of those years.

4. Turnover Ratio
    We strive for a 6 to 10 error ratio. In 15 seasons our opponents have averaged slightly over 17 errors per game while we have averaged slightly over 9. In every season the opponents have made more turnovers.

5. Foul Ratio
    We strive for a 6 to 10 foul ratio. In 15 seasons our opponents have averaged slightly over 21 fouls per game while we have averaged slightly over 12. In every season the opponents have committed more fouls.

The POSSESSION SCORING PERCENTAGE FORMULA is a simple formula devised to add a closer evaluation of this defense. Briefly, you divide the number of team points by the number of ball possessions by the particular team. The final figure is called the Possession Scoring Percentage or PSP.

Thus, we add the total number of field goal attempts, free throw attempts, and turnovers (cupping the ball, traveling, double dribble, charging, bad pass, 3-second violations, 10-second violations, etc.) and divide by the number of points scored by the team. We set a goal to have a plus .75 PSP and to hold our opponents below .60 PSP.

In Diagram 1-1 versus Muncie Central we had 61 goal attempts, 23 free throw attempts, and were guilty of 9 turnovers. This adds up to a total of 93. So you would divide 93 into the actual team points scored (67) and get a PSP of .72, which is close to what we strive for. Our opponent had 65 field goal attempts, 11 free throw attempts, and 15 turnovers. This adds up to 91. So by dividing 91 into their actual score of 56, you get a PSP of .62.

GAMES 22	FINAL SEASON AVE. PSP (ANDERSON HIGHLAND) .74						FINAL SEASON AVE. PSP (OPPONENTS) .59					
	OPPONENTS						ANDERSON HIGHLAND					
School	Score	Errors	FG Att	FT Att	Total	PSP	Score	E	FGA	FTA	T	PSP
Muncie Central	56	15	65	11	91	.62	67	9	61	23	93	.72
Elwood	46	8	54	14	76	.60	64	11	56	18	85	.75
Madison Heights	53	13	53	5	71	.75	55	9	55	23	87	.63
Tournament Frankton	32	13	54	7	74	.43	65	4	57	11	72	.90
Tournament Semi Pendleton Heights	45	24	42	19	85	.53	55	8	50	23	81	.68
Tournament Championship Lapel	62	11	63	18	92	.67	67	12	50	35	97	.69
Taylor	31	26	53	20	99	.31	73	8	60	18	86	.85
Yorktown	53	14	63	5	82	.65	61	14	50	11	75	.83

A Partial Possession Scoring Percentage Chart Summary for a Season

Diagram 1-1

The PSP gives a clearer picture of total game performance and can also be broken down to indicate individual player performance. For instance, if a player had 12 field goal attempts, 6 free throw attempts, committed 4 errors, and scored 22 points, he would have a very good PSP rating of 1.00.

The INDIVIDUAL PLAYER EVALUATION CHART is depicted in Diagram 1-2. This is an individual game chart that gives each player the positive and negative aspects of his performance by touching on the finer aspects of the game that we stress. This chart can also be used in daily practice sessions.

At the bottom of the chart is a cumulative total section, readily indicating who did the job and who did not. We have found that this chart keeps the players on their toes, as it sometimes tells why a boy is benched during the game or loses a starting position. It also works in reverse. It may show a nonstarter doing a better job than a starter, hence implying that maybe strong consideration should be shown in this area. It is a great aid for a coach since it gives a broader view of the game.

TEN DEFENSIVE COMMANDMENTS

Our defenses has held 192 of 392 opponents under 50 points per game and has a 15-year defensive average of 47.3. We have held our opponents under 50 points per game in 12 of 15 years. In our "worst" season defensively, we allowed 54.7 points in 24 games.

We set up the following goals in our early years of coaching and still live by them today. They are called the TEN DEFENSIVE COMMANDMENTS. We feel that if the ten goals are successful or even nearly successful, victory should be achieved even with a poor offensive effort!

1. Minimize the opponent's PSP.
   As explained earlier, the goal is to hold the opponent under a .60 PSP.
2. Minimize the opponent's number of field goal attempts.
3. Minimize the opponent's percentage field goal attempts.
   The goal is to keep the ball outside the perimeter and stop any penetration.

Game No. 24 Anderson Highland vs. Carmel	#24 Egger	#20 A. Richie	#34 Poole	#14 Sanders	#30 Lantz	#22 Cook	#12 T. Richie	#10 Jamerson	#44 Kessler	#42 Knotts	#33 Cupp	#40 Holton	
Offensive Rebounds													+2
Defensive Rebounds													+2
Assists													+2
Steals													+1
Tieing ball up													+1
Taking a charge													+2
Baskets made													+2
FT made													+1
POSITIVE PTS.													Total
Errors													−1
Fouls													−1
Missed Shot Att.													−1
Missed F.T. Att.													−1
Missed 1-1 F.T. Att.													−1
Not back on defense													−1
Failing to front													−1
Not having hands up													−1
Beaten on screen													−1
Beaten Weakside Rebound													−1
Did not blockout													−1
Leaving feet improperly													−1
Not getting baseline													−1
Not stopping penetration													−1
Defensive lapse													−1
NEGATIVE PTS.													Total
POINT TOTAL													

Cumulative Point Totals

Number	Pts.		Number	Pts		Number	Pts.
#24			#30			#44	
#20			#22			#42	
#34			#12			#33	
#14			#10			#40	

Diagram 1-2

4. Minimize the opponent's fast-break baskets.
   You must hustle back on defense when the ball is lost. All five players have to get down the floor and get there immediately. The best weapon against a fast break is a defensive fast break!

5. Minimize foolish defensive mistakes.
   Eliminate such defensive errors as leaving the feet on ball fakes, not having hands up, not taking the baseline, not stopping penetration, getting beat on a screen, not fronting a man, not getting back on defense, etc.

6. Minimize cheap baskets.
   You must eliminate all second shot possibilities, establish a good weakside position, and strive for a 10 to 8 rebound ratio.

7. Minimize foolish fouls.
   Strive to keep the opponent under 15 free throw attempts per game. Shoot for a 6 to 10 foul ratio.

8. Minimize your opponent's scoring efficiency.
   Strive to hold the opponent under 50 points per game. We have held 192 of 392 opponents under 50 points and have won 188 of the 192 under 50 games.

9. Minimize your opponent's field goal accuracy.
   Hold the opposition under 40% accuracy. In 15 years we have allowed a 37.4% average with the highest yearly average being 39.3%

10. Minimize the opponent's ball-handling efficiency.
    Strive for a 6 to 10 turnover ratio. In 15 years we have averaged slightly over 9 per game while the opponents have averaged slightly over 17.

RECENT SUCCESSES OF THE MAN/ZONE

A few years ago I served as a player-coach of a semi-pro team that used the Man/Zone exclusively and posted a 31–0 record, winning two league and five tourney championships.

In my first head coaching job, we used the Man/Zone and its derivatives and over a three-year period won three conference and three tourney titles by posting a 75–12 record. We set a school record, holding a team to 17 points and unofficially led the state one season in defense at 46.8 per game.

Later, I took over a program which had never won a league championship. The previous year resulted in a 2–22 mark. In two years we posted a 47–12 record, a berth in the state finals, and the school's first league title. The team was number one in 1972, set a school record by holding a team to 19 points, and set a team season record by allowing only 47.8 points per game. Again the Man/Zone played a major part.

Later, we returned home to Indiana to coach one season at North Judson High School. The Man/Zone and its derivatives led the team to a 20–4 record and first Conference title in the school's history. The team finished 7th in the state on defense with a 51.8 average.

At Anderson Highland High School (Anderson, Indiana), I took over a program that had won only 35% of its games in the 18 year history of the school. Highland had never won a postseason tourney, won only one conference title, and had a longest winning streak of only four games! We installed the Man/Zone and in a four-year period posted a 78-13 mark, including four conference titles, a 25-game winning streak, the school's first Sectional and Regional titles, and a perfect 20–0 season record. We set a school record by holding a team to 8 points! We also led the state in team defense twice and finished second one other year. Our best state-wide ranking was number two.

Over a 10-year period at four different high schools, the Man/ Zone has played an integral part in posting an overall 220-41 mark, numerous conference and tournament titles, plus state-ranked teams in Illinois (#1) and Indiana (#2).

A majority of the time, this was accomplished with shortages in height and talent. I might add that in all four schools, although height and talent were indeed limited, we were blessed with kids with extreme dedication and desire that helped to make up for other deficiencies.

PRO'S

We consider the following to be positive factors in using an aggressive Man/Zone type defense:

1. Players do not have to be as talented to run a zone-type defense.

2. Players are always in relatively the same positions.

3. A player can be at liberty to gamble if the coach so desires, because he usually has a backup player.

4. It is effective against a pivot attack, since it generally closes normal passing lanes.

5. It is an excellent defense if the floor space is narrow.

6. It is ideal for the fast break.

7. A team with a strong defense "knows" it will be in every game.

8. It can lead to the development of good team unity.

9. You can place your best rebounders underneath. You never have to worry about a mismatch unless it is already there.

10. It stops the driving, screening, one-on-one type of game.

11. You can play uncoordinated players who could not play a man-to-man defense.

12. It develops aggressiveness and hustle in stealing the ball.

13. It forces the opposition to play a different game than the one they usually want to play.

14. It can be a psychological weapon against certain players who fear zones (also some coaches who fear zones) and hurry or force their play.

15. It reduces foul trouble. You can hide a player by changing his defensive position.

16. It can help to control the tempo of a game. It breaks the opponent's rhythm.

17. It can enable strong two-timing of individual star players.

18. Many teams have poor attacking zone offenses.

19. Each man can be held liable for scoring done in his zone or area.

CON'S

We consider the following to be negative factors in using an aggressive Man/Zone type defense:

1. It *does not* conserve energy.

2. It requires excellent teamwork

3. It requires players in tip-top condition.
4. It tends to weaken individual responsibility as no matchup of players according to height, speed, and ability takes place.

PLAYER POSITION REQUIREMENTS AND BASIC SLIDES

POINT (X1): Must play his man in area head on and not let him penetrate the defense . . . must keep eye on ball at all times . . . is captain of defense and must pick up his man and others follow . . . first objective is not to allow shot in his area; second objective is to stop a high post pass; 3rd objective is to stop penetration . . . when possible, block out his man first before rebounding . . . slide in a straight line and not a loop.

WINGS (X2 and X3): When not playing man with ball, should sink off men in direction of basket . . . speed and anticipatory ability will vary and this affects the distance of sagging (sag off man as far as you can, but still be able to get within an arm's length when he gets the ball) . . . acts as a backup man for point (X1) . . . keep eyes on ball at all times . . . when ball is in corner and you are the weakside wing you must rebound tough because you are only defensive man on weakside . . . must call "cutter" or "man-through" to alert teammates when a man is cutting through the defense . . . turns his body toward the ball when it is out front, putting one hand toward the highpost area and the other hand toward the man in the wing area . . . slide in straight line and not a loop . . . first objective is to stop wing shot; second objective is to keep the pass out of the middle; third objective is to stop penetration . . . when possible, block out his man first before rebounding.

POSTMEN (X4 and X5): Do not give up baseline unless you are in "force baseline defense" . . . when a weakside postman, sometimes acts as a backup man for strongside postman . . . sometimes acts a backup man for wings and occasionally the point on pivot penetration on dribble or pass . . . should be best rebounders . . . must be skilled in fighting screens on baseline . . . also skilled in never leaving feet on ball fakes . . . can turn sideways to keep vision on their zone sometimes and not face ball . . . when possible, block out his man first before rebounding . . . keep eyes on ball at all times . . . must front everyone within 8 feet of basket . . . cannot be flat-footed or back on heels . . . must keep turning the head to see action on either side . . . slide in a straight line and not a loop . . . do not play too low or close to the goal.

All defensive basketball teams are only as good as the individual ability of each player. Ideal attributes are speed, alertness, pride, desire, aggressiveness, and anticipation. The following defensive fundamentals are vital to the success of the Man/Zone:

ARM ACTION: The primary aim is to cause a poor pass. Move arms around in a jerky windmill fashion. Do not try to steal the ball and *don't* foul. By keeping the hands up high, more passes are attempted in a floating manner.

STANCE: Should be wide and close to the defensive man. This forces the dribbler to go wide, and if he doesn't he will probably be called for a charging foul. Knees should be kept bent at all times so a player can move quickly. Your weight should always be between your legs—never over either one. With one foot ahead and one behind, you have already gained a step toward your opponent or toward the goal. With this stance it is very easy to move forward or backward. Right-handed players seem more comfortable with the left foot forward and vice versa. The closer together the feet are, the less balance the player has. Hips and buttocks should be low to maintain a low center of gravity, and the head, shoulders, and back should be in a straight line and stationary. The key to aggressive defense is to keep moving. Your movement may be backwards or sideways, but your weight should still be evenly balanced. You cannot afford to sit back on your heels or your man will beat you.

TALK: Talk is essential regardless of the type of defense employed. In developing the Man/Zone, we feel talk is a most vital element.

While lecturing at coaching clinics, I mentioned the importance of talk in defensive basketball. During the question and answer period at each clinic, coaches stated: "we would like to get our players to talk but do not know what to have them say." This indicated a need for each coach to develop meaningful terminology, not just idle chatter, that would be beneficial to his players.

Players who are in the postman positions or who find themselves on the weakside two passes from the ball, are in a great position to help their teammates with talk.

Some of the "terms" you may find helpful are:

Get the baseline, Dave!

Watch out behind you, Rick!

Who's got the corner, Mike!

Man through! (cutter through zone)

Hit the boards, Brian!

Ball! Ball! (when ball is loose or recovered)

Pick right, Adrian! (on a screen)

Watch that screen, Tom!

Front him, Kimpy!

Keep the hands up, Bruce!

Don't lunge—get back, Greg!

Don't get too far under, Scott!

We have found the Man/Zone defense gives more outside coverage than any other zone defense. In setting up the defense, begin by establishing the "no man's land" area. It is one that extends from one foot from the top of the free throw circle, or approximately 22 feet, to each corner as illustrated in Diagram 1-3. Unless facing an outstanding outside shooting team, we would let any offensive player shoot from anywhere outside this area. Thus, we try to shut off any penetration inside the 22-foot area, and hence the name "no man's land."

The starting position for the Man/Zone defense is depicted in

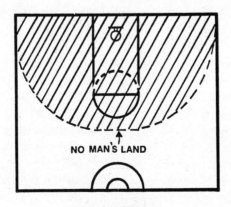

Diagram 1-3

Diagram 1-4. X1 takes a position on top of the free throw circle, approximately 22 feet from the basket. X1 can adjust his position to the outside shooting ability of the offensive man or men in this area.

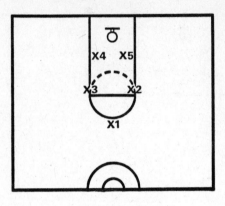

Diagram 1-4

If the offensive man is a weak shooter, X1 can sag off him and help in the high post area. X2 and X3 take a position at the 15-foot free throw stripe extended with one foot in the lane. Again X2 and X3 can sag off the man in their area as far as they can, and still be able to get within an arm's length when he gets the ball. The speed and anticipatory ability of X2 and X3 will vary and this affects the amount of sagging. Another factor would be the outside shooting ability of the opponent. X2 and X3 must turn their body towards the ball when it is out front, putting one hand toward the post and the other toward the man in the wing area. A primary objective is to keep the initial pass of the offense out of the high post area. X4 and X5 take a position approximately seven feet in front of the basket and about a step into the lane. In this position they should turn sideways to keep vision on their zone and should not face the ball. They should keep turning their head side to side to be aware of anyone cutting behind them.

In the diagrams we have the offense moving the ball to the right side of the floor. The moves of the defensive men would be the same if the ball goes down the left side of the floor with X2 and X3 and X4 and X5 exchanging responsibilities.

Diagram 1-5 shows the position of the Man/Zone when the ball is moved to the right wing position. X2 must hustle out (we tell our players to charge out like maniacs) and be at least within an arm's length of the offensive man by the time he receives the pass. An

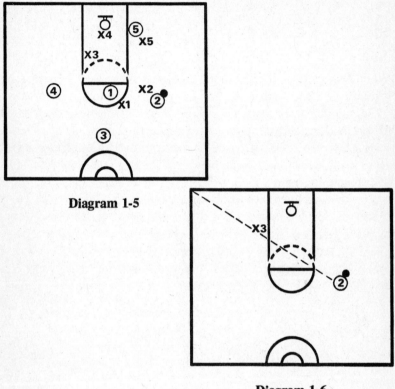

Diagram 1-5

Diagram 1-6

important coaching point here is to have X2 move in a straight line towards the offensive man without looping. He must defend closely with a wide base, approximately left shoulder to right shoulder, while using his hands to intimidate the offensive man. X1 drops to approximately X2's original position, fronting anybody in this area. In Diagram 1-5, X1 is depicted fronting player 1. X3 takes a spot inside the foul lane, at a spot between the ball and the weakside corner. This will keep X3 content as to how far he is to sag. Too often a player in this position will sag too much or not enough. The proper sagging technique is illustrated in Diagram 1-6.

X5 cheats towards the right corner and X4 moves over in "unison" with him, maintaining the same distance. If there is no offensive man in the corner, then X5 can stay closer to the foul lane. In practice, we have on occasion tied a rope around both players' (X4 and X5) waists so they learn that when one of them moves in one direction the other must move also.

Diagram 1-7 illustrates the Man/Zone movement when the ball is passed to the right corner. X1 still fronts anyone in his area and moves deeper down the foul lane. X2 moves to a position in an imaginary line extended from X1. X2 and X5 are responsible for stopping all penetration attempts by player 5. X5 hustles out on the pass to 5 and makes sure he is at least an arm's length away when the ball arrives. He also charges in a straight line and defends closely with a wide base, using his hands for intimidation purposes. Besides stopping penetration with X2, he is solely responsible for stopping the baseline drive of 5. We tell our players they may have to swing the left leg (on the right side of the floor) on the endline to force the offensive man away from the baseline. X4 moves over to a position directly in line with X5 and must front anyone in this area. Also, if X5 is beaten on the baseline then X4 is the backup man.

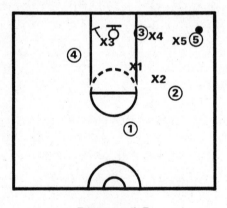

Diagram 1-7

X3 plays approximately in a straight line with X4 and X5, about one to three feet to the side of the basket. In case of a high lob over X4 to offensive player 4 (Diagram 1-8), X3 is responsible for stopping 4. A good defensive player in this position will often draw a charging foul on 4. X3 must also crash the boards hard because in this case he is the only weakside rebounder. Often your wings are not your bigger players, so you may have 5'6" to 5'10" players rebounding at this spot against the 6'4" to 6'10" players. We have had 5'6" players play this position, and play it well. We have films of players in the 5'6" range out-rebounding 6'6" or even bigger players by hard work and determination.

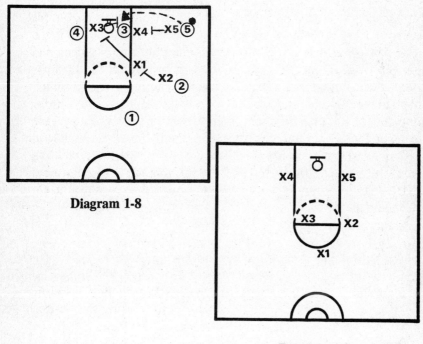

Diagram 1-8

Diagram 1-9

Since most right-handed teams and players go to the right in their offensive patterns, as a variation you may start with an unbalanced alignment. The same lineup and slides can be used to the left side if it were determined that the offense had a tendency to go left.

As illustrated in Diagram 1-9, X1 starts approximately 22 feet from the basket at the top of the free throw circle. X1 adjusts his position with the outside shooting ability of the offensive man or men in his area. X2 overshifts to a position one to three feet outside the lane at the free throw stripe extended. X3 overshifts to an initial position in the high post area. Your two toughest and best defensive players should be in the X2 and X3 positions. X2 and X3 have to bust hard and cover the most territory in this setup. X4 and X5 are your two best rebounders and normally your biggest players. X5 takes a position about five feet in front of the basket and about a step outside the lane. X4 takes a position about 5 feet in front of the basket and a step outside the lane on the left side. X4 may never have to cross the lane except in emergencies and remains primarily a weakside rebounder. X4 and X5 should turn sideways to the ball in order to maintain good vision on their zone area.

As depicted in Diagram 1-10, when the ball is moved to the right wing, X1 moves back and fronts anyone in the right high post area. X3 fronts any offensive player in the middle lane area. X2 plays the ball and hustles out, and should be at least an arm's length away by the time offensive player 2 receives the pass. X2 moves in a straight line towards the man and does not loop. He must defend closely with a wide base, while using his hands to intimidate the offensive man. X4 moves a few steps and stays as the weakside rebounder. X5 moves halfway to the corner, if the opponents have a man in the corner. If there is a low post man in this area it would be X3's man and X1 would sink deeper in the lane.

When the ball goes to the corner as in Diagram 1-11, X1 slides low by the dotted circle fronting anyone in this area. X3 shifts as low as the low post offensive man. He must establish a fronting position on his man. X2 sags back to keep the ball out of the middle. X4 remains stationary, ready to crash the boards on the weakside. X5 hustles out and takes the offensive man in the corner, making sure he is within an arm's length of the man when the pass is received. He also defends closely with a wide base, using his hands to intimidate. X5 is the primary defender of the baseline with his backup man being X3.

When the ball is reversed all the slides are the same, and if it goes down the left side the same responsibilities hold. If the opposition reverses the ball quickly or sets a screen on X3 as in Diagram 1-12, the following minor adjustments take place. You simply have X4 take the spot that would normally be X3's and have X3 slide over to X4's spot. X1, X2, and X5 use their normal slides. If the

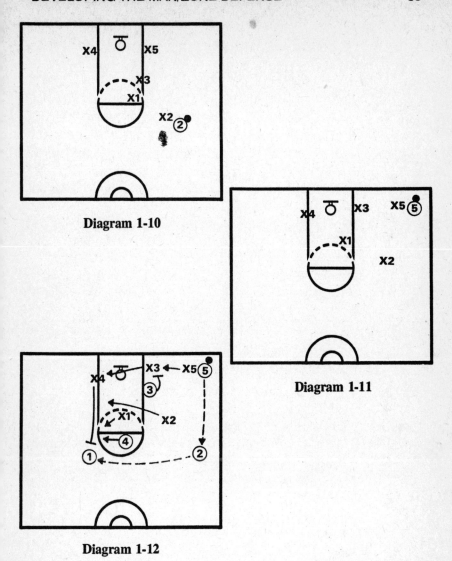

Diagram 1-10

Diagram 1-11

Diagram 1-12

ball moves back out to the top of the key, X4 and X3 can exchange back to their original lineup. If the defense would be overshifted to the left side and the ball is quickly reversed to the right side, the two players who might switch would be X5 and X2. Our special, pivot coverage adjustments and other variations will be discussed in detail in Chapter 4.

RULES IN TEACHING THE MAN/ZONE

We issue the players a mimeographed copy of the following Man/Zone rules and go over four or five rules per day at early practice sessions.

1. Never guard space—look for an area to help.
2. Never give up the baseline—unless you are in the "force baseline trap series."
3. Everytime the ball moves you move. Keep your eyes on the ball at all times.
4. Never let the opponent get the ball inside. Always front the opponent within 8 feet of the basket (if possible and feasible, within 12 feet).
5. Do not double-team (two or more players trapping the ball) unless you are in a trapping defense. Exception is when a pass penetrates the middle.
6. Postmen can stand sideways occasionally to maintain better vision on their zone.
7. Crash the weakside rebounder slot hard. Normally there is only one defensive rebounder in this area.
8. Pressure the ball hard within 22 feet of the basket with a wide stance. Whenever an offensive man is within scoring distance and has the ball, the defensive man must be within an arm's length of him. The player should slide in a straight line and not loop.
9. Hands must be up at least shoulder height at all times and high in a windmilling fashion when pressuring the ball.
10. Do not leave your feet on a fake shot or ball fake. Blocking shots, or trying to, is a risky business unless you have superior height and timing. It's better to concentrate on trying to keep the man in your area from getting the ball than it is to try and block his shot after he gets the ball.
11. Don't lunge and hope for the best in attempts to steal the ball. This helps to break down the defense and often times puts your teammates in a 4 versus 5 situation.
12. Be ready to help a teammate if he is beaten by the opponents.
13. Talk is essential, especially on screens and cutters.

14. The wing players (X2 and X3) play man defense on a dribble to the corner from the wing position.

15. The weakside wing should retreat to a position in line with the ball and the weakside corner for a good rebounding position.

16. Do not let the dribbler penetrate. You must stop all penetration into the 22-foot ''no man's land.''

17. Fight over all screens over the top.

18. Understand all rebound responsibilities and block out. When possible, block out your man first before rebounding.

19. Use two or three retreat steps and try to force a cutter wide, yelling out ''cutter'' or ''man through.'' This helps to clog the area and prevents a give and go move.

20. You must hustle back on defense and stop the opponent's fast break.

SPECIAL DRILLS

The following drills have proven successful in teaching the Man/Zone defense (also review the 20 rules listed in the previous section when using these drills).

Deny the post-pass drill (Diagram 1-13)

Offensive players 1 and 2 have no defense on them and they look for 3 and 4 who have X4 and X5 on them. Three and 4 can

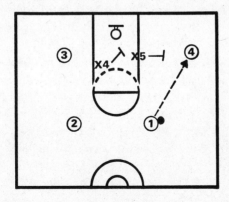

Diagram 1-13

break towards the ball to meet the pass, switch positions with each other, or flash to the high post. X4 and X5's primary objective is to guard 3 and 4, but they also help out each other if either X4 or X5 is beaten by their offensive men one-on-one or backdoored. The weakside man must sag and help.

Man through drill (Diagram 1-14)

When the offensive player cuts to the basket as 1 is doing in Diagram 1-14 after passing to 5, the defensive man in this area (X2) must go with him two or three retreat steps toward the basket. He should yell "man through" or "cutter." Then X2 should stay in this area to clog up the middle until a new offensive player (2) replaces 1. The reason for the two or three retreat steps is to prevent a possible give and go pass.

Stop the drive drill (Diagram 1-15)

You do not want the ball to be penetrated on a dribble between any two Man/Zone players. Diagram 1-15 depicts offensive players 1, 2, and 3 against X1, X2, and X3. The defense must stop an attempted drive by any of the three offensive men, an attempted drive and a quick backpass to an offensive man for a jumpshot, and a possible backdoor cut by one of the offensive men if his defensive man is sagging to stop a drive or is playing a weakside sag position. In the diagram, 1 attempts to drive and is stopped by X1 and X3, 2 is using a backdoor cut and must be covered by X2, and 3 is available for a backpass and a jumpshot and would have to be covered by X3.

Destroy the screen drill (Diagram 1-16)

As illustrated in Diagram 1-16, use six offensive men against the Man/Zone and use screens on the postmen, wings, and point. In 1-16, offensive players 4 and 6 are setting screens for player 1. X4 and X5 must fight the screens and work in unison with the weakside post (in this case X4 hustling over to front 6). The strongside post-man (X5) must cover the cutter coming around the screen, but cannot leave the screener until another defender (X4) tells him to. If X5 leaves, without "help" player 6 is wide open. Use normal Man/Zone slides with the weakside wing sagging, etc. If possible, fight over the top of the screen with one or two quick steps and try to keep the hand nearest the goal in front of the screener.

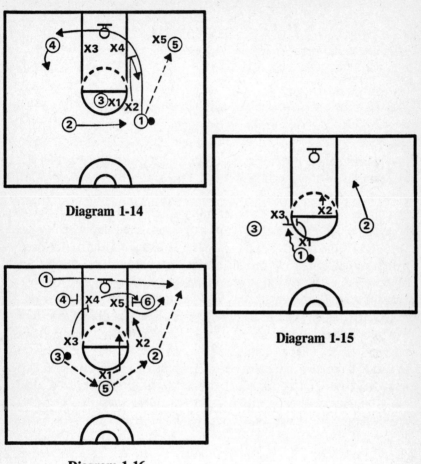

Diagram 1-14

Diagram 1-15

Diagram 1-16

Situational game drill

We go live 5 on 5 half-court and score the game this way:

1. We play the game to 25 points
2. Offense scores:

   regular ways (1 point—free throw, 2 points—basket) of-fensive rebound—1 point

3. Defense scores:

gain possession of ball (steal, error, etc)—1 point, knock ball out of bounds—1 point, fast break from a rebound and score—2 points

King of the hill drill (Diagram 1-17)

As illustrated in Diagram 1-17, the player named first on the Round Robin schedule receives the ball first. The contest is a one-on-one affair and besides being primarily used as a defensive drill, is also excellent in helping a player learn individual offensive moves.

The defensive player starts the contest by giving the ball to the offensive man at the free throw line. The offensive player has two options—shoot or drive to the basket for a close shot. If the offensive player scores or misses the shot and secures his own rebound, he gets the ball again and is allowed to shoot a free throw. This puts pressure on the defense to (1) play tough defense and (2) block out and rebound tough. If he makes the free throw he gets another offensive one on one turn. If he misses, the defensive man gets the ball and the offensive man goes to defense. Free throws do not count in the score as only baskets count 1 point. The first player to garner 3 points is the winner. By requiring the free throw, we put extra pressure on the player and also help our free throw practice. You will find the games are usually very spirited and highly competitive as most boys have a great deal of pride in one-on-one competition.

Another restriction in the game is that the offensive player is allowed only 6 dribbles in making his move. If he should use more than six dribbles he forfeits his turn and goes to defense. There also cannot be any backing in as this would be unfair, for example, to the 7-foot player versus the 5'5" player. The game is also played without boundary lines and contests are held at each of the six baskets.

The player with the best record at the end of the 11-day schedule is awarded the King of the Hill award which is usually a milkshake. The player who wins the match writes the score in the appropriate space on the chart.

As examples in Diagram 1-17, you can see that player 6 defeated player 9 by a 3-1 score at basket one. At basket two, player 12 defeated player 3 by a 3-2 margin. At basket three, player 4 beat player 11 by a 3–0 score, etc. In each instance the winning player would mark the score in the appropriate space.

	1	2	3	4	5	6	7	8	9	10	11	12
1												
2												
3												
4											3-0	
5												
6									3-1			
7												
8												
9												
10												
11												
12			3-2									

PLAYERS

1	2	3	4	5	6	7	8	9	10	11	12
POOLE	EGGER	A RICHIE	COOK	KNOTTS	LANTZ	SANDERS	T RICHIE	HOLLON	CUPP	JAMERSON	KESSLER

ROUND ROBIN SCHEDULE

Basket

1	6-9	11-3	5-8	10-11	12-8	4-2	8-1	9-3	4-7	7-12	1-9
2	3-12	10-4	2-11	9-12	4-5	5-12	9-7	6-1	3-8	6-2	10-8
3	4-11	8-6	12-1	8-2	3-6	7-10	10-6	7-5	1-11	9-10	2-5
4	5-10	9-5	6-7	1-5	2-7	6-11	2-3	8-4	12-10	4-1	3-4
5	2-1	1-7	3-10	6-4	10-1	8-9	12-4	11-12	2-9	5-3	11-7
6	7-8	12-2	4-9	7-3	11-9	1-3	11-5	10-2	5-6	8-11	12-6

Diagram 1-17

ANALYZING SHOT CHARTS

A chart used for games (and for practice sessions on occasion) is the Defensive Shot Chart illustrated in Diagram 1-18. We want to know where the scores are made and why. We give particular attention to second shots (follow-ups). We post this chart at half time and also may discuss it at the next practice session following the game.

In Diagram 1-18 it is evident that our left wing was not doing the job in the first quarter. Our opponent had secured three weakside rebounds on three corner shots from the right side, two going for baskets. The opponent had five offensive rebounds so we were having a lot of trouble on the defensive boards. It also indicated that our right post had been scored upon three times from the right corner. The opposition had scored two other baskets on an un-molested layup (probably from a steal) and a jumper from the left wing position. Overall, our defensive performance in this quarter was poor since we allowed six shots within the 22-foot area and the opposition had made 7 of 16 first quarter shots. This chart gives a better look at the defense than the normal shot chart.

This was our first quarter of a game with Anderson, a team ranked fourth in the state. Obviously, with such a poor defensive effort, a good offensive show would be needed to balance the quarter. We made 11 of 14 shots (78%) for a 22–16 first stanza lead. Coincidently, this game was our worst defensive game of the year, as we yielded a season high of 71 points. In contradiction to the theme of this book, the offense won this battle as we made a phenomenal 30 of 46 field goal attempts (65%) while Anderson made only 33 of 86 in our 84–71 victory. This example of a poor defensive effort has been used on purpose to show that it takes a tremendous offensive effort to turn the tables of victory. A team would probably win just a few games by allowing the opponents 40 or more shot attempts as in this example!

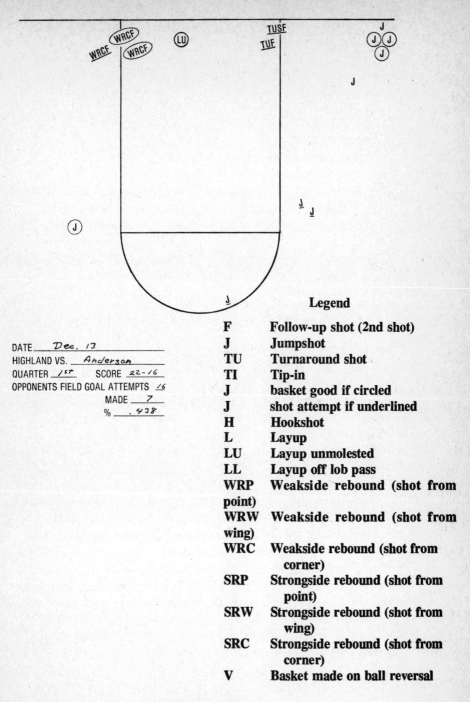

Legend

F	Follow-up shot (2nd shot)
J	Jumpshot
TU	Turnaround shot
TI	Tip-in
J	basket good if circled
J	shot attempt if underlined
H	Hookshot
L	Layup
LU	Layup unmolested
LL	Layup off lob pass
WRP	Weakside rebound (shot from point)
WRW	Weakside rebound (shot from wing)
WRC	Weakside rebound (shot from corner)
SRP	Strongside rebound (shot from point)
SRW	Strongside rebound (shot from wing)
SRC	Strongside rebound (shot from corner)
V	Basket made on ball reversal

DATE___*Dec. 13*_____

HIGHLAND VS. ___*Anderson*_____

QUARTER __*1ˢᵗ*___ SCORE __*22-16*__

OPPONENTS FIELD GOAL ATTEMPTS __*16*__

MADE ___*7*___

% ___.*438*___

Diagram 1-18

Example in 1-18: WRCF means it was a basket on a weakside rebound follow-up on a shot from the right corner.

2

ATTACKING VARIOUS OFFENSES WITH THE MAN/ZONE

Recently we played a conference opponent that had a reputation of losing very few games on its home floor. The outdated gym was very small and dimly lit and the opposition also had a reputation of hiring biased or "homer" officials.

In 21 years our school had never won a game on this floor. Despite the adversities we were playing a respectable ball game, but because of the poor lighting we were unable to see the score on the old-fashioned scoreboard. So I called a timeout and asked one of the referees over. "I can't see the scoreboard," I said. "What's the score and how much time is left?" The referee answered: "There's one-minute 25 seconds to go and WE ARE ahead by three points!"

If you ever get in this predicament, especially with all the high-powered offenses of today, you had better have a good *defense* to get you through the night!

We depend on our scouting reports, and if possible prefer to see a team at least three times before we play them. We keep individual files on each team from year to year. Through the use of scouting reports we are usually able to work against the opponent's offense during practice.

We usually have our sophomore and junior team (B-team) run our opponent's offense and we walk through our various slides and the possible options the opponent may have. Then we go live. If the opponent were to attempt to "surprise" us by playing an entirely different offense from the one that we had scouted, we would still feel adequately prepared because each week we also work against varying offenses.

This section will illustrate how the Man/Zone handles some of the popular offenses that have been used against it. We have broken the offenses down into two categories—those whose initial setups start with two guards and those that start with a lone guard.

Some of the various attacks other coaches and teams will try to use to defeat the Man/Zone are listed below:

1. Break to the gaps:
    Each offensive player will try and sense the open area or the gap and cut to that spot. A player will probably cut to the ball and then away if not open.

2. Reverse the ball to weakside and keep wingman wide:
    The offense will try good ball reversal and will usually keep the offensive man in the weakside wing area wide.

3. Penetrate the Man/Zone:
    The offensive man may dribble through a gap in the defense for a layup or drop off a pass close to the basket. He may cut and come out on either the ballside or the weakside.

4. Try to penetrate the pivot area:
    The offense will try to keep pressure on both the high and low post areas. Any pass or dribble penetration severely hampers the defense.

5. Rotate behind the give and go man:
    After the give and go man cuts to the basket, a player

who is between him and the ball should time his cut looking for the open area.

6. Give and go:
   The offensive man will try to pass and break for the basket, hoping to be open momentarily for a return pass. He will cut and come out on either the ballside or the weakside.

7. Will try to crash the offensive boards:
   Some offenses will try to put two offensive men on the weakside after a shot.

8. Will try to use short, quick passes and not high floating or lob passes.

9. Will try to fast break the Man/Zone:
   Teams will try to get down the floor before the Man/Zone can set up.

10. Will try to screen the Man/Zone in all defensive areas:
    The offense may try to create screens from the strongside and weakside and are quite prevalent in the baseline area.

11. Will try to throw the cross court pass and the "skip" pass:
    Some teams will use the cross court pass for a sneak weakside basket. We played one squad that actually had a set play where they would ricochet the ball off the backboard to the weakside for a surprise basket. A "skip" pass is to skip offensive players offensively to defeat a sag on defense.

12. Will try to produce a mismatch:
    The offense may try to create mismatches by placing their big man on the weakside rebound slot. They also might place "mismatch" personnel in the gaps of the defense and not head on.

13. Will try to make cuts to the ball from behind the Man/Zone.

14. Will try to distort the Man/Zone with an overload offense.

15. May try to hold the ball to bring the defense out if tied or ahead:
    I used to be a detractor of the proposed 24- or 30-second shot clock for high school basketball. The use of a slow-

down in the later stages of a game is good strategy, but unfortunately some coaches make a mockery of the stall and a few coaches may even try for "actionless" games. This is unfair to (1) the spectator (2) the players themselves and (3) the opposing coaching staff. I would now favor a 30-second shot clock for high school play.

THE MAN/ZONE VERSUS VARIOUS TWO GUARD OFFENSES

For the sake of brevity, the following actions are standard in each Man/Zone defensive sequence against the various offenses:

1. All arm action is a high, windmilling type when pressuring the ball and semi-high when away from the ball.

2. All defensive slides to the ball are done in a straight line and not a loop.

3. All defensive players must arrive on the offensive man on the ball by the time the ball arrives and be no farther away than an arm's length (when the opponent is within scoring distance.)

4. The player on the ball must arrive in a wide stance.

5. All players must front their opponent within 8 feet of the basket if possible and within 12 feet if feasible.

6. When collapsing to the ball on a pass within the pivot area, the player collapsing must use an upward, swinging movement of his arms and not stab downward.

7. Postmen may stand sideways occasionally to maintain better vision of their defensive area.

8. Use two or three retreat steps and try to force a cutter wide, yelling out "cutter" or "man through." This helps to clog the area and helps prevent a give and go move.

Review the twenty rules in Teaching the Man/Zone listed in Chapter One while going over the defensive slides versus the various two- and one-guard offenses which follow.

In all Man/Zone player movements in the diagrams in this chapter the original starting position is depicted in Diagram 1-4.

VERSUS STACK OFFENSE: The initial alignment for the Man/Zone varies somewhat as X3, as depicted in Diagram 2-1, sags deeper against the stack. As in 2-1, if 2 is successful in a pass to 3 in the highpost area (if X1 and X2 are alert the pass will not be successful since the first objective is to keep the initial pass out of the middle) X4 will come up on the pass and defend 3. X1 immediately collapses to the ball moving his hands in an upward, palms-up motion to deflect the ball if possible and helps double-team the ball with X4. If X1 moves his hands in a stabbing downward motion he is more susceptible to fouling and most officials tend to call more fouls in these cases. X3 is alert to possible passes to 4 or 5. X5 sinks to a position directly behind X4 and approximately five feet behind X4. X2 sinks to the basket and is alert to cover 2 who is breaking to the lowpost area. X5, X3, and X2 are responsible for 4, 5, and 2 as X4 remains with 3 until 3 releases the ball.

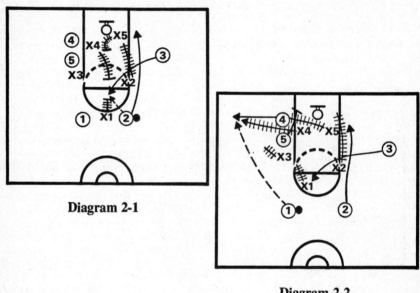

Diagram 2-1

Diagram 2-2

In Diagram 2-2 if 1 makes a pass to 4 in the corner, 4 is immediately covered by X4. X5 moves "in unison" with X4 and covers 5 in the lowpost. X3 sags approximately 4 feet from X5 and is also ready to help in the lowpost area. X1 sinks in the lane and clogs the middle and is aware of a possible move to a gap position by 3. X2 sags to the weakside and remains alert as 2 is breaking to the weakside lowpost area.

VERSUS 2-3 OFFENSE: As illustrated in Diagram 2-3, X1 has 1 and retreats two or three steps on 1's pass to 3 and yells "cutter" or "man through" (Rule #19) to alert his teammates and prevent a give and go pass. X2's original position can be deeper and he slides out to take 3 as 1 is absorbed into a pocket by X1 and X5 so he cuts to the right corner. X5 moves over and looks for 1 cutting into the lowpost area and also is aware of any weakside cutters, possibly 5. X4 clogs the lane in the middle and X3 sinks to a weakside position in the lane even with an imaginery line between the ball and the weakside corner. X3 is also aware of a possible cross court pass to 4 who is breaking to the highpost area.

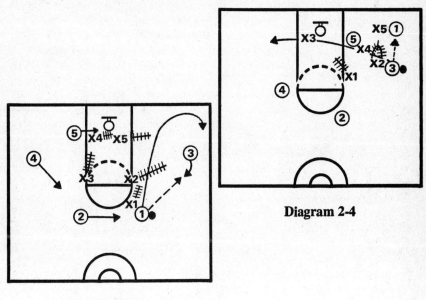

Diagram 2-4

Diagram 2-3

In Diagram 2-4 when the ball is passed from 3 to 1 in the right corner, 1 is covered by X5. X4 fronts anyone in the lowpost and helps to clog up the lane as 3 cuts through in a give and go move. X2 retreats a few steps and initiates Rule #19. X1 sinks in the lane almost directly behind X2. X3 sinks to the weakside almost directly in a straight line with X4 and X5. If a cross court pass were made out to the top of the key area to 4, X1 would be responsible for covering the pass and the other 4 players would adjust back to almost their initial positions.

If the ball would be reversed to the weakside, the players would shift back to near their original positions. For instance if the ball were passed 4 at the highpost (Diagram 2-5) to 3 now in the left corner X4 would slide over to take 3. X5 would front in the lowpost area and would be alert to 5's cut across the lane and 4's cut through to the weakside. X3 would invoke Rule #19 in trying to clog the lane for 4. X2 would drop to the weakside approximately in line with X4 and X5. X1 would move to his normal ball in the corner position almost directly behind X3.

VERSUS 2-2-1 OFFENSE: As illustrated in Diagram 2-6, X2 slides and covers 3 on the pass from 1. X1 fills X2's position, being aware of 2 moving over to the top of the key area and also in a fronting position of the highpost area that may be penetrated by 4.

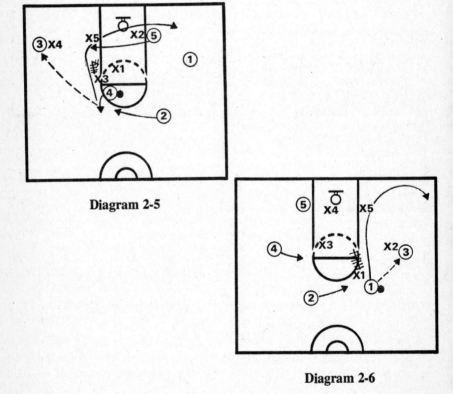

Diagram 2-5

Diagram 2-6

X1 also initiates Rule #19 on 1 as he cuts through the defense. X3 sinks to a position on the weakside in a direct line with the ball and the weakside corner. X5 moves over a step or two to clog 1 in his cut and is also ready to defend 1 in the corner if 3 decides to pass to the right corner. X4 moves over to the middle of the lane and is aware of 5 in the deep left lowpost.

Three reverses the ball to 2 and the players return to their initial defensive appearance. As 2 passes the ball to 5 (Diagram 2-7), X3 moves over to cover 5. X1 fills X3's position and fronts 4 who moves down the lane in the highpost. X4 slides left and is ready to cover 1—first in the lowpost and second if 1 continues on to the left corner and receives a pass from 5. X5 slides to the middle of the lane and if 5 does pass to 1, X5 moves over to front in the left lowpost area. Four may decide to drop further down the lane and would be picked up by X5. X2 moves on the pass to 5 in a line between the ball and the weakside corner. If 5 does pass to 1, X2 moves deep on the weakside and approximately in a line with X5 and X4. X1 and X3 sag and help in their areas if necessary.

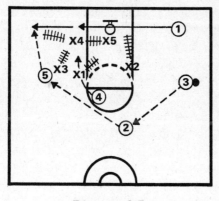

Diagram 2-7

VERSUS 2-1-2 OFFENSE: In Diagram 2-8 on 1's pass to 4, X5 slides over to pick up 4 and X4 moves over to front in the right lowpost area. Four is especially aware of 5's move to that area. X2 also sags to help in this area and is ready to take 3 or clog the lane as 3 looks for a possible gap in the lane area. X1 sags to the highpost area and is aware of 1 circling through the highpost and replacing 2.

X1 is also ready to defend 2 if 4 reverses the ball. X3 sinks to a deep weakside position.

If the ball is reversed to 2, all 5 players shift to spots near their original starting positions. As shown in Diagram 2-9, 2 passes to 1 and X3 would slide forward to pick up 1. X1 would fill the left highpost position covering 1 on his cut to the opposite guard's spot. X1 is also aware of a possible cut to the highpost area by 3. X2 retreats a step and is ready to help in the highpost area if necessary and also the right lowpost if needed. X4 moves over to the left lowpost area and is ready to defend 5 as he comes across the lane. X5 moves over to the middle of the lane.

If 5 goes to the left corner and receives a pass from 1 as in Diagram 2-9, 5 is covered by X4. X3 moves down the lane and is ready to help out in the high lowpost area and is especially aware of a cut to the gaps from the weakside by 4. X5 slides across and fronts anyone in the left lowpost area and is also aware of 4. X1 sags in the lane to help if necessary and is approximately four feet behind X3. X2 sinks to the weakside area in a line with X4 and X5.

For many years, stationary offenses were acceptable in attempting to beat your opponent. Recently, many teams have used a rotating type offense. More recently, teams have leaned towards a picking type defense to defeat zone-type teams.

PICKING OFFENSE: In Diagram 2-10, 5 breaks to the highpost and screens X1. If X1 is unable to get over the screen as in Rule #17 (if X1 is tough he will get over), X2 must come up a step or two and stop 1. As 3 drops to an area between X2 and X5 trying to split them, X5 moves up a few steps and is ready to defend 3 if the pass goes to 3. X4 moves across the lane and is ready to defend 4 as he crosses the lane. X3 sinks on the weakside to a position in line with the ball and the weakside corner. X3 will be responsible, once the ball passes the rightwing area, for 4 in the left lowpost area (before 4 comes across the lane) and also 5 as he rolls down the lane on the weakside. X1 fronts in the highpost area and also is ready to defend 2 if necessary.

THE MAN/ZONE VERSUS VARIOUS ONE GUARD OFFENSES

VERSUS 1-3-1 OFFENSE: In Diagram 2-11, on the pass from 1 to 2 in the wing position X2 slides out and covers him following Rules # 8 and #9 as listed in Chapter 1. X1, X2, and X3 team up

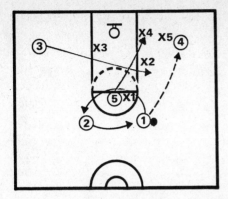

Diagram 2-8

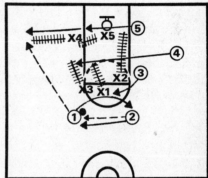

Diagram 2-9

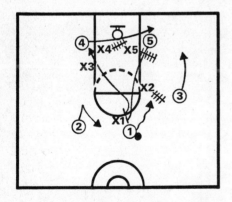

Diagram 2-10

to keep the initial pass out of the middle. X1 fills X2's spot and temporarily fronts 3. X3 sags to a weakside position directly in a line between the ball and the weakside corner. X4 slides over a few steps as does X5. X5 is aware of 3, in case 3 moves to the lowpost, and is ready to move out and cover 5 if the next pass goes to the corner.

In Diagram 2-12, 2 passes to the corner and then cuts to the basket in a give and go move. X2 retreats a few steps and exercises Rule #19. X2 comes back a step and is ready to defend 1 if the ball is quickly reversed. On occasion we let X2 play in the passing lane to prevent a reverse pass. X1 sags a few slides deeper to clog up the area. X3 sinks to a deep weakside position almost directly in a line with X4 and X5 and is ready to help out on cutter 2 or give X4 help if needed. X5 bursts out to cover 5 in the corner and arrives as the ball gets there and exercises Rules #8 and #9. He makes sure he is not beaten on a baseline drive. X4 moves over and is a backup man for X5 and covers the lowpost area and will front 3 as he moves down the lane from the highpost. X4 also can receive help from X2 if 3 shoots for a gap between X4 and X2. If 5 attempts a pass over X4 to 3 and is successful, it would be X3's job to stop 3. X1, X2, and X4 all collapse to the basket in this situation.

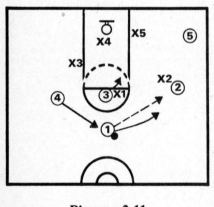

Diagram 2-11

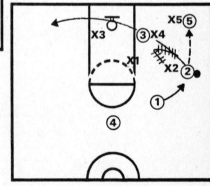

Diagram 2-12

VERSUS WISHBONE OFFENSE: This is an offense developed by the author (*Basketball's Wishbone Offense*, Parker Publishing Company, Inc., West Nyack, N.Y.) that gives the Man/Zone more trouble than any other over the years.

In Diagram 2-13 the Wingman Cutback Option which leads to the Baseline Series is depicted. On the pass from 1 to 2 to the rightwing position, X2 slides out and takes 2. X1 drops to a spot behind X2 jamming the lane. X3 sags to the weakside directly in line with the ball and the weakside corner. As soon as he sees 3 making a loop to the middle, X3 yells "cutter" to alert his teammates. X3 then uses a few retreat steps to jam the cutter. X4 cheats a step or two forward to jam the middle also, but is still aware of 4 who may break to the basket. X5 moves over a few steps and is ready to help in two ways in the lowpost area and to cover 5 if the pass goes to the right corner.

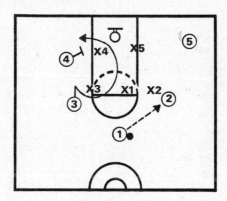

Diagram 2-13

In Diagram 2-14, as ball is reversed to 1 the players return to near their original positions. As 1 dribbles to the left to initiate the Baseline Series, X1 slides a few steps with 1 and X3 also comes over to help if necessary. X4 moves to a fronting position on 4 and is ready to cover 3 if the pass goes to the corner. X5 comes over quickly, helping to jam cutter 3. X2 drops to the weakside in line with the ball and the weakside corner. He is well aware of 5's position.

On 1's pass to 3 in the left corner, X4 covers 3 as X5 works in unison with X4 and replaces X4 in fronting 4. X3 drops deeper in the wing area and is responsible for a quick backpass to 1 in the wing area. X2 drops to approximately a direct line behind X5 and X4. X1 sags in the lane and is alert for a cross court pass to 2 or he may help out in the lowpost area if 5 should break across the lane.

In Diagram 2-15, 3 reverses the ball to 1 and 1 is covered by X3 in the wing area. All other players slide back to approximately the same positions as when the ball was at the wing. X4 yells "baseline" as 3 starts his move to the opposite corner. As the ball is passed from 1 to 2, X1 picks up 2 and the rest of the players slide back to approximately the positions they held when the ball was at the point position.

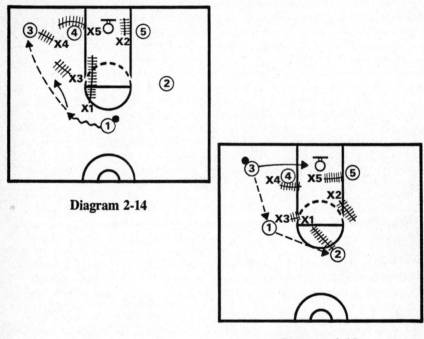

Diagram 2-14

Diagram 2-15

As illustrated in Diagram 2-16, the complete Baseline Series option of the Wishbone is completed as 3 breaks to the right corner. If the ball were passed to 3, the slides depicted in 2-16 are just the opposite as when the ball was in the left corner.

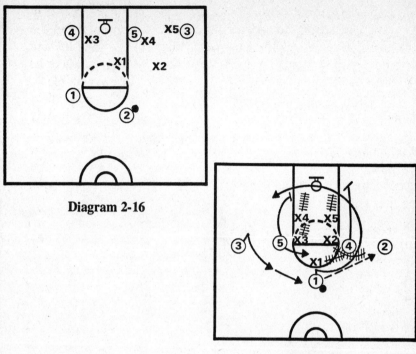

Diagram 2-16

Diagram 2-17

VERSUS 1-4 OFFENSE: As shown in Diagram 2-17, X2 and X3 will adjust to a side position on 5 and 4 and X5 and X4 move approximately five feet higher than normal in the lane area against the 1-4 offense. All five Man/Zone players must be especially alert against this formation because in the initial offensive set you have one defensive man responsible for two offensive men in two areas. One passes to 2 and X2 slides out to cover 2. X1 fills X2's position and fronts 4 temporarily while yelling "cutter." X1 tries to jam 1's cutoff of 4. If 2 would dribble to the corner X2 would go with him. X3 sags a few steps but is alert to clog up the middle if 5 would cut there. X4 and X5 drop 3 or 4 steps and are alert for cutters. One rolls off of 4 and must be picked up by X5 as he makes his cut for the basket. Two attempts a give and go pass with him if possible. If 1 doesn't receive a pass, he continues across the lane still looking for a possible pass from 2. X4 now is alert for possible action on 1. If there is still no pass to 1, 1 continues off a block by 5 who has dropped to the lowpost. As soon as 1 makes his cut across the lane, 4 breaks to a lowpost position and must be covered by X5.

The final sequence is illustrated in Diagram 2-18. If 1 has continued off 5's block to the left corner he is covered by X4, and X5 moves over to front 5 in the lowpost replacing X4. X3 sags to a position approximately three feet from the lane and helps in the lowpost if necessary. X1 fills the approximate spot X3 left and is about 4 feet behind X3. X2 sags to the weakside and is aware of 4 in the right lowpost area on the weakside. X2 is almost in a direct line with X4 and X5.

VERSUS DOUBLE LOW STACK OFFENSE: As illustrated in Diagram 2-19, X2 and X3 play three or four feet deeper than normal when you face the Double Stack offense. X1's job is to keep 1 from penetrating and must try to make him go as wide as possible. X1 will go as far as 2 feet outside the lane, but then he becomes X2's property and X1 sags slightly and is responsible for the high-post area that 3 is breaking to. As an alternate, X1 may go with 1 until he gives up the ball and X3 would come up to the highpost. X2 will play between 5 and 1, but when X1 drops off 1, 1 becomes X2's main responsibility. If 5 moves up a couple of feet and receives a pass from 1 over X2, 5 is picked up by X5 and 2 would collapse to the ball. Two becomes X4's responsibility and X3 sinks to the weakside and is responsible for 4.

As shown in Diagram 2-20, if 1 would pass to the right corner to 2, X5 would slide out to cover him and X4 would front 5 in the lowpost. X2 would sink to a position two feet outside the lane. X3 would sag deeper on the weakside, almost directly in line with X5 and X4. X1 would sag deep in the lane area almost directly behind X2.

Diagram 2-21 illustrates the action when 1 gets a pass inside to 3 as 3 is breaking to the middle. X4 bursts up to stop 3 and X1 collapses to the ball helping X4. X5 slides directly behind X4 and is ready to defend 2 or 4 in the lowpost area if necessary. X3 and X2 sink immediately to the basket and help. X1 and X4 stay with 3 until he releases the ball. If 3 makes a backpass to 1, the players would return to nearly their original positions.

VERSUS THE SHUFFLE CUT OFFENSE: As depicted in Diagram 2-22, on 1's pass to 2, X2 slides over to cover 2. X1 fills

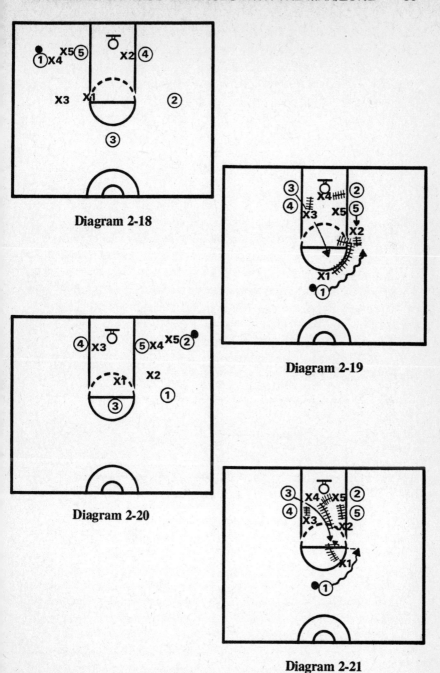

Diagram 2-18

Diagram 2-19

Diagram 2-20

Diagram 2-21

X2's position and clogs the lane, being aware of 5 who is screening in the highpost. X3 drops in the lane and helps and is approximately in a direct line between the ball and the weakside corner. X5 fronts 4 in the right lowpost area and X4 moves to the middle of the lane, but still is aware of 1 who after a shuffle cutoff of 5 may be trying to sneak behind the defense in the left lowpost area. If 4 moves towards the corner, X5 cheats out on him and X4 moves over to front the lowpost, being aware of 5 rolling to the lowpost area. If 5 does not get the ball in the right lowpost area he will slide across to the weakside and must be covered by X3. If the ball is reversed to the weakside and is at the point position, the players return to their normal starting positions.

In Diagram 2-23, the ball is passed to the left corner to 5 and 3 is cutting through the lane off 4's highpost screen. X4 covers 5 in the corner and X5 fronts the left lowpost area looking for 4's roll to that area. X2 is on the weakside and helps jam the lane, and is aware of 3 cutting through the lane to the right lowpost area. X3 sags off 1 as 1 passes the ball to 5 and helps in the lowpost if needed. X1 moves near to X3's vacated position, and if 4 does not receive the ball in the left lowpost he will slide across to the weakside area and must be covered by X2.

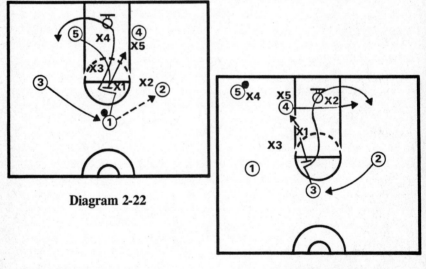

Diagram 2-22

Diagram 2-23

3

UTILIZING THE FULLCOURT PRESSURE DEFENSES

Pressure defenses, now at a zenith of popularity, are best defined as a means of advancing, attacking tactics by a forcing defense. Zone pressure is in most instances better than man-to-man pressure, as one good dribbler can defeat the man-to-man pressure, as one good dribbler can defeat the man-to-man defense. A weak man-to-man player can even be beaten by a dribbler who is only fair.

Two important factors for winning basketball games are defense and taking advantage of the opposition's weaknesses. A pressure pressing defense will take advantage of these two elements. Often overlooked is the basic weakness of basketball players. Playing against a pressure defense is a common weakness that many players possess.

There are many factors involved when considering whether to press or not and the coach has to decide when to use it and when to call it off. If a team doesn't have depth and may be subject to committing fouls and doesn't have good team speed or quick reactions, a coach may decide it would be foolish to press except under emergency situations. I have used the press in every game in some seasons and only when necessary in others. There are some coaches who will not use pressure even when they fall behind late in a game.

The press allows some boys to play that could not participate under so-called normal defenses. The press demands desire and dedication. Speed or quickness surely help, but hard-nosed players with a good sense of anticipation can become excellent pressure defense disciples. Some of our best pressers have not been fast but made up for it with these other qualities. You must have a high degree of cooperation, because each player must know exactly where his teammates will be in each situation. The players must talk to each other constantly. This is very important, but unfortunately very hard to accomplish. Most players practice their offensive skills with little or no defensive pressure. Because of this fact, I don't believe that many players are prepared to operate effectively on offense against a good pressure defense.

We tell the players the opposition may get three to six easy baskets a game, but if the press is well executed it should double that number of points by interception and easy layups. This type of defense cannot be taught in a few days or weeks. It requires at least a month or more for players to learn its basic uses. Then through constant practice it becomes part of the regular defensive pattern. Team press characteristics include speed, aggressiveness, anticipation, concentration, cooperation, dedication, desire, alertness, and most of all long, hard practices. Each player must do his job and do it to the best of his ability. No player can afford to loaf. If one player cannot handle his requirements, the entire effectiveness of the press is lost. In a zone press you can cover up for a weak defensive man more than you can in a man-to-man press. It is my belief that practicing and playing pressing defenses more thoroughly develops basketball ability in the individual player than almost any other method known.

Our concept of the press entails the following: (1) to tire our opponents, (2) to make interceptions, (3) to force turnovers, and (4) to disrupt the opposition's offensive pattern.

REASONS FOR A PRESSING DEFENSE

The press is no longer reserved just for the final minutes of a game when a team must catch up. It's being used for the entire game and in various forms. All things being equal, the effectiveness of a press depends largely on its use at the right time. We may use the press because of the following reasons:

1. As a game saver: You should always make a move when things are going bad. If your offense can't get going or is running out of gas the press can be a game saver. I can recall a game where we trailed by 23 points in the second quarter. We switched to the press and finally won the game by three points. In the finals of a tournament one season we trailed by 13 points at the end of the third quarter. We rallied with the press and won on a last second basket.

2. To control game tempo: When combatting the slow break or set play team, the press can be effective in ruining the opponent's timing and speeding up the game tempo. Squads at all levels possess great shooters. By consistent harassment you can limit a shooter's effectiveness. Also, against the "running" opponent the press can bother the rebounder, slow up the outlet pass, and stall the running attack.

3. Versus the inexperienced team: To combat the press, slow and inexperienced squads must possess sound fundamentals, but most inexperienced teams lack these necessary skills.

4. Versus the great offensive postman: The press can be a great equalizer. You can't score without the ball so keep the postman from getting it, or force him to receive the ball away from his normal scoring range. Against a squad with a great height advantage the press can be an equalizer. Recently we were in the finals of a sectional tournament. Our opponents featured a 24–2 mark and averaged 6'6" across the frontline, while we averaged only 6'0" in our forward wall. Besides the great height advantage, our opponents were averaging nearly 80 points per game and featured a fine fast break. We

realized that to win we had to apply full court pressure to keep the ball away from their inside strength as much as possible. To make a long story short, our opponents committed 29 errors, becoming so frustrated that they actually hit the backboard on three occasions on the inbounds pass. They also managed to score only 52 points as we rolled to a convincing win and a trip to the semistate.

5. If our squad possesses superior manpower over an opponent, we may force the undermanned team to go at top speed. Unfortunately we haven't had this "problem" on many occasions in my years as a coach.

6. As a "no-foul press": We are ahead by 1 or 2 points late in the game. Our opponent has the ball in backcourt after calling a timeout to set up strategy. The opponent must fight the time clock to score, so make him use some of the precious time combatting a "no-foul" type of press.

7. If it is known that a team has a good press, an opponent will often spend a great deal of practice time preparing to combat that defense, necessarily neglecting other drills. Our team at Elgin was in this mold. We had a statewide reputation because of our pressing tactics. Many coaches would confide to me that they would spend endless hours at practice preparing to defeat our "devastating press." Almost all of the schools on our schedule possessed a great height advantage, so we used all types of pressure to combat our disadvantage. We pressed every game with a full-type zone to start the contest and then possibly adjusted to other forms of court pressure. An excellent pressing unit, along with the Man/Zone defense, proved to be a major factor in a 25–3 season plus a berth in the coveted state finals. The "reputation" of the press played a vital role!

8. As a surprise move: The press can be a great psychological weapon. Teams, even good ones, sometimes panic when they see a press they are not expecting.

9. Many teams are coached to slow up and set up when they reach mid-court; you can press and they will wait for you to set up your defense. What more can you ask?

10. Versus a freeze or stall team: Forcing tactics must be employed to combat the "stall" team. If we are behind

late in the game and hope to win, we must successfully combat this technique.

11. It forces teams in poor condition to move more, and therefore they are more prone to turnovers.

12. A majority of close games are won in spurts: A press at the opportune time may lead to a brief spurt. A good example of this came in an all-star game. As in many all-star games the halfcourt zone defense was outlawed. We decided to use a full-court zone press if necessary. Trailing by a couple of points with just over five minutes remaining, we used the press for a 15-point "spurt" and a 109 to 96 victory.

13. It blends with an aggressive offense as it leads to many interceptions, turnovers, and various misplays that lead to quick baskets.

14. While shooting is improving (the field goal percentage is the highest today in the history of basketball), the quality of ball handling seems to be decreasing. If possible, press!

15. It makes a more interesting game for the fans because they usually prefer fast action.

REASONS FOR NOT USING A PRESSING DEFENSE

1. A pressing defense may give up easy baskets as it involves anticipation and taking chances while the defense is widely spread.

2. It is tiring and all players must be in excellent condition.

3. Players are susceptible to fouls.

4. The breakdown of one player tends to kill a pressure defense.

5. Pressure defense takes a high degree of cooperation and teamwork.

6. Your team may lack overall anticipation, aggressiveness, speed, or team depth. Except under special situations it would be foolish to press.

SPECIAL "LEAD-UP" DRILLS FOR A PRESSURE DEFENSE

The best method to use in teaching any type of a press is to start with the basics and develop into the more complex phases of the game. The pressure defense must be carefully organized, sold one hundred percent to the players, and drilled on daily.

As a practice suggestion, divide your main floor into three areas. You can run three different drills in these areas for a period of 5 to 6 minutes. After this time period each drill group will rotate right (or left) until each drill is completed.

For example, in the lead-up drills below the 2 on 1 trap, call trap, triggerman, and stop the dribbler could be held in area two while the other drills could be divided up in areas one and three. Of course, the two fullcourt drills are Drills 1 and 9. (See Diagram 3-1.)

1. TWO VERSUS EIGHT
   One and 2 try to advance the ball the length of the court through the four areas. The two defensive men in each area try to steal the ball. They may play defense only in their area. The players rotate with the two X's in area one, going on offense, and the other X's move up one area. One and 2 take over defensive positions in area four. (See Diagram 3-2.)

2. TWO ON ONE TRAP DRILL
   Players X1 and X2 are on defense. Offensive player 1 cannot dribble. He may move around but he must maintain a pivot foot. The two trappers move to take the ball away without fouling. The player who gets the ball by deflecting it, prying it or tying up the offensive player in a jumpball situation then goes on offense against the other two.

3. "CALL TRAP" DRILL
   Players 1 and 2 pass the ball back and forth over X1 and X2. They are approximately ten feet apart. When the manager (M) yells "Trap," X1 and X2 must trap player 1 or player 2. (See Diagram 3-3.)

4. PRESSURE ON TRIGGERMAN DRILL
   We put X1 on the ball guarding player 1. X1 varies his distance from right on the ball to a position 3 or 4 feet from the baseline. Player 1 attempts to pass to M (the manager). (See Diagram 3-4.)

5. STOP THE DRIBBLER DRILL
   X1 starts approximately 15 feet from player 1. X1 should meet the offensive man, stop him, and force him to pivot.

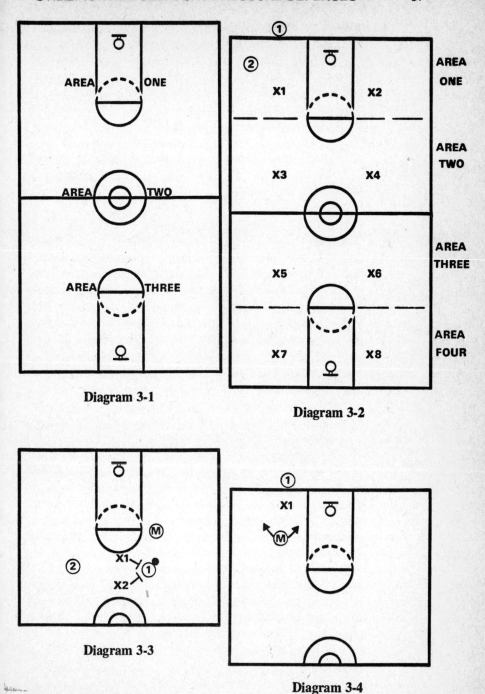

Diagram 3-1

Diagram 3-2

Diagram 3-3

Diagram 3-4

6. TWO ON TWO ON BALL
X1 guards triggerman 1 tightly and when 1 releases the ball X1 yells "Ball." That tells X2 who is overplaying player 2 with his back to the ball that the ball is in play and he should react to the situation. (See Diagram 3-5.)

7. THREE ON THREE
Same drill as #6, but with a third offensive and defensive player added. The offense can only move from the baseline to the top of the key area as denoted in the diagram by the dotted line. All kinds of offensive maneuvers can be utilized, such as picking, crossing, etc. (See Diagram 3-6.)

8. FOUR ON THREE
Same drill as #7 with a fourth defensive player (X4) added in the midcourt area. The offensive players are allowed to move 30–35 feet from the baseline. X4 attempts to pick-off all long passes. (See Diagram 3-7.)

9. STOP THE LONG PASS DRILL AND RECOVER
X1 guards player 1 at the free throw line. Player 2 throws the long pass to player 1 and X1 attempts to break up the pass. If the pass is successful, X1 must hustle to the endline to keep 1 from scoring. (See Diagram 3-8.)

10. TWO ON TWO FORCE TO SIDELINE DRILL
X1 must stop player 2 on the sideline and X2 comes over to form a double-team. The immediate objective of the trap is not to steal the ball. If player 2 who is in possession of the ball carelessly hangs the ball out for the defense, we want our players to stab at the ball, without fouling, for a quick steal. On most occasions we want the defense to force the offense into a bad pass. X1 and X2 should maintain a close position and wedge the offensive player into a "V." They must make use of their hands and arms in harassing the offense. We want the trapper to spread out in a wide base as he makes his last step to trap. He should place his foot nearest his teammate (X2) close to that of his teammate to prevent the offensive player from going between them. What we hope for is a stolen pass, a deflected pass, a five-second call (in frontcourt), or a ten-second call in backcourt. (See Diagram 3-9.)

11. GOALIE DRILL
We put the goalie on defense at the free throw line and then run 2 on 1, 3 on 1, 4 on 1, and even 5 on 1 situations

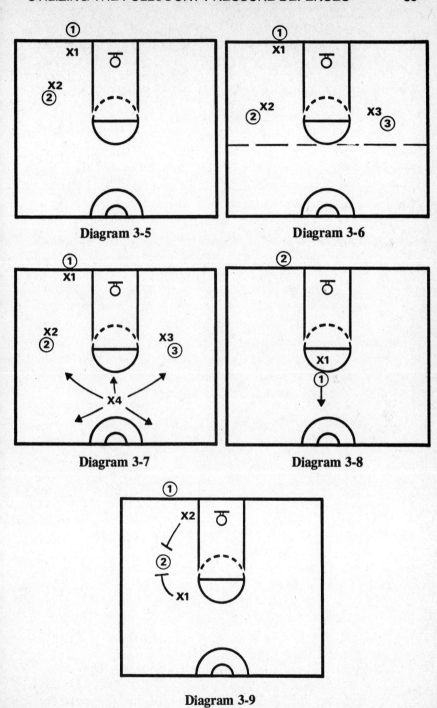

Diagram 3-5

Diagram 3-6

Diagram 3-7

Diagram 3-8

Diagram 3-9

on him. It is the goalie's job to absolutely not allow the layup if possible and to delay the offensive maneuvers until help arrives.

NUMBER AND COLOR CODES FOR PRESSURE DEFENSES

Over the years we have used various methods of "identifying" the various presses. We do this to simplify matters so that we can make a quick change on the court without calling a timeout or without "tipping off" our changes by yelling from the bench. Some of our methods of signalling different defenses will be explained in another chapter. Our favorite method will be detailed here.

We simply divide the court up into one-fourth sections with 100 meaning fullcourt on the ball pressure, 75 for three-quarter pressure at the free throw line extended, 50 for midcourt pressure, and 25 for halfcourt pressure. We also give each of the presses a color code, such as blue, red, orange, green, white, etc. For example, in the next section we will describe the fullcourt pressure defense which we label with a green color. Thus, if we say Green 75 everyone knows we are in the three-quarter court pressure defense. If we call Green 50 we are in the midcourt trapping defense and if we say Green 25 we are in a trapping formation from the quarter court area. (See Diagram 3-10.)

NICKNAMES AND PLAYER POSITION REQUIREMENTS

We also give the players nicknames so everyone can identify with a position easily. Following are the player position requirements and nicknames for the five positions:

PINCHER . . . traps with Chasers . . . usually on ball or closest player to ball . . . can be a big player . . . should be fairly quick and a good trapper . . . tallest player we have had at position was 6'7" and the smallest 5'10".

RIGHT AND LEFT CHASERS . . . usually around 15 feet in back of the Pincher on the left and right sides . . . normally trap with the Pincher and occasionally with Rover and Goalie . . . usually the shorter and quicker players on the squad . . . tallest player we have had at this position was 6'7" and the smallest 5'8" . . . the Chasers may interchange with the other three positions.

ROVER . . . usually behind the Chasers 12–25 feet . . .

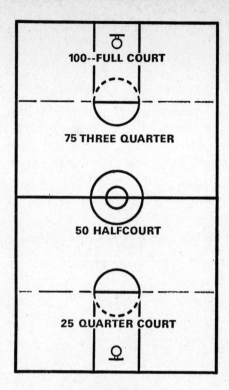

Diagram 3-10

should have excellent anticipation and savvy . . . tallest player we
have had at this position was 6′3″ and the smallest 5′8″ . . . the
Rover normally rotates position with the Goalie but may also interchange with the other positions.

GOALIE . . . usually responsible as the last line of defense . . . normally the tallest and slowest player on the squad . . .
tallest player we have had at this position was 6′7″ and the smallest
5′9″ . . . the Goalie normally rotates with the Rover but may also
interchange with the other positions.

THE FULLCOURT PRESSURE GREEN 75 DEFENSE

We position our players as in Diagram 3-11. The philosophy in
this type of pressure is to let the opposition bring the ball to us. The
Pincher stays at the free throw line extended and tries to force the

ball to one side or the other. The Left and Right Chasers position themselves in the backcourt area, approximately 15 to 20 feet in back of the Pincher. The Chasers will not come up to set a trap with the Pincher until the ball handler has passed the free throw line extended. When the ball gets to this area the Chaser and the Pincher set an immediate double-team. The Rover located in the forecourt area, approximately 15 to 20 feet behind the Left Chaser, should come up to help cover anyone in the middle. In Diagram 3-11, for example, the Right Chaser also has responsibilities on the middle area if the offense places a man here. An important teaching point here is to be sure that the players on the trap keep their hands up so the opposition cannot make sharp, direct passes.

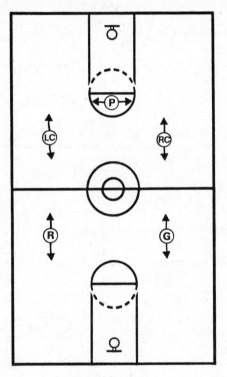

Diagram 3-11

As depicted in Diagram 3-12, if the opponents get by the original trap the Rover must come up to stop the ball and the Left

Chaser slides back to trap with the Rover. The Pincher now slides back towards the middle looking for a possible interception. The Right Chaser now sprints back to the top of the key area in the forecourt and assumes goalie duties. The Goalie rotates to the original Rover position. All players should slide anticipating the pass into the press.

We allow the opponents to pass back and hope that they do! It eats up time and the opposition seems more anxious to pass into the press. As in Diagram 3-13, the Pincher must arc back to the other side to keep a pass from going directly to the middle and give the other players time to shift to their area. Players should shift back anticipating a pass into the zone. As Diagram 3-13 shows, on the backpass from player 1 to player 2 the Pincher and the Right Chaser will now double-team as player 2 attempts to get the ball down the

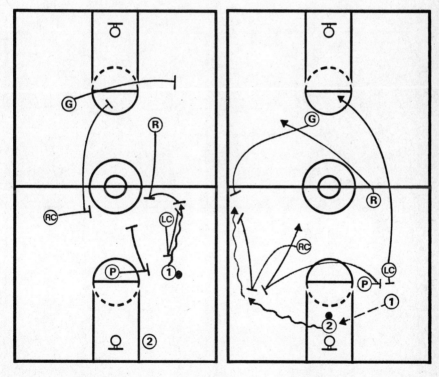

Diagram 3-12   **Diagram 3-13**

sideline. If player 2 is able to beat this trap, then the Goalie should come up and stop 2's dribble and the Right Chaser would join the Goalie in a doubleup. The Pincher would slide back into the middle of the press looking for an interception. The Left Chaser sprints back looking for a possible steal and assumes goalie duties. The Rover rotates to the original Goalie position on the strongside. If the opponents get by this trap, another possible double-team may occur with a rotation with the Rover now double-teaming with the Goalie as in Diagram 3-14. The overall complete rotation would now be the Right Chaser to the middle replacing the Pincher, the Left Chaser replaces the Rover (in the original Goalie position), and the Pincher rotates to the Goalie position. I might add that the press seldom rotates to this stage as usually two or three double-team situations are the limit, either because of a gain in possession of the ball or a score by the offense.

As depicted in Diagram 3-15, if the offense does get the ball to

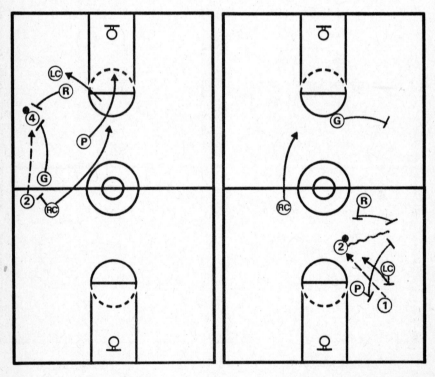

Diagram 3-14   Diagram 3-15

the middle of the press we have the backman, in this case the Rover, come up and stop player 2's dribble or stop him by driving him to the sideline. Do not let him drive down the middle! The Pincher should drop back and try for a steal or double-team with the Rover.

If the pass is made across the court, say from player 2 to player 3, shift as shown in Diagram 3-16. The Right Chaser is responsible for sliding over and stopping player 3, forming a double-team with the Pincher who must hustle over from his position on the now weakside of the floor. The Rover slides into the middle of the press replacing the original Left Chaser. The Left Chaser rotates to the Goalie position and the Goalie rotates over by returning to his original position.

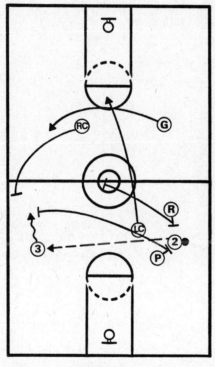

Diagram 3-16

ADJUSTMENT TO TRIGGERMAN GREEN 100

A possible adjustment to make would be to place the Pincher on the player with the ball out of bounds (the triggerman). This would be the Green 100 formation as depicted in Diagram 3-17. The Pincher must wave his hands and yell at the ball handler trying to distract him. Usually the idea is to prevent the long inbounds pass. The pincher must also observe where the passer is standing in regard to the backboard overhead. If the ball handler is under it, he cannot pass high so the Pincher can concentrate on the short pass. If the passer is to the left of the backboard but close to it, he will be unable to pass high to the right, etc. Normally, the Pincher must pressure the passing arm of the man out of bounds. The other pressers, especially the Rover and the Goalie, should watch the ball handler out of bounds. If he has a square stance with the ball in two hands, the pass will generally be a short one. If he turns so that he has one foot in front of the other and the side of his body to the court, he will generally try to throw the long, bomb-type of pass. The movement of the eyes is another passing tip-off.

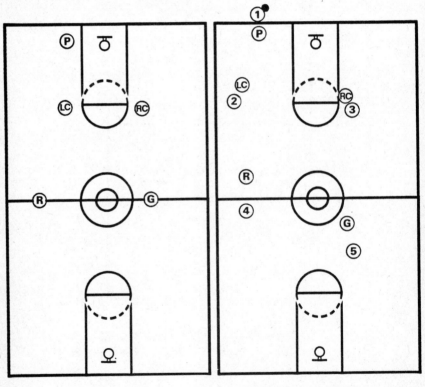

Diagram 3-17   Diagram 3-18

The Chasers would also move up to approximately the free throw line extended. The Rover and the Goalie would move in accordance with the movement of offensive players in the midcourt or forecourt areas. As an alternate change of pace defensive maneuver, either the Chasers, Rover, or Goalie may match up with the opponents as in Diagram 3-18 and overplay, facing the opponent back to the ball. If the offense successfully inbounds the first pass, then the original Man/Zone pressure slides are applied.

PRESSURE FROM SIDELINES INBOUNDS PASS

When the ball is passed in from the sidelines, as in Diagram 3-19, we still use the press if we so desire. We usually press on the sidelines inbounds pass with all of our full- and three-quarter (100 and 75) presses. Diagram 3-19 shows an example of our Green 75 press from the sideline situation. Occasionally we have found that this tactic comes as a surprise to the offense, as a few teams have a

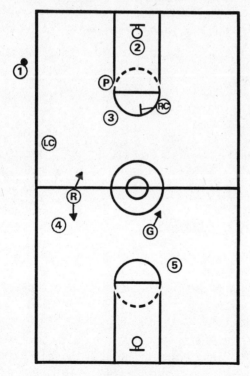

Diagram 3-19

fullcourt pressure offense but not an organized offense from the sideline.

PRESSURE FROM A MISSED SHOT
WITH INTERCHANGEABLE POSITIONS

With pressure defenses, we will on occasion press even after a missed shot, getting right into the press regardless of player alignment. This may or may not be necessitated by the interchanging of player positions. For example, the pressure nearest the ball becomes the Pincher, the next two pressers become the Chasers, etc. As described in Diagrams 3-20 and 3-21, as the ball is rebounded by offensive player 5 the closest presser to him, the Goalie, now becomes the Pincher, the Right Chaser and the Rover become the Chasers, the Left Chaser becomes the Goalie, and the Pincher becomes the Rover. Of course, in this type of setup the player alignment depends solely on where the ball is exchanged from offense to defense and also which pressers will the Pincher, Chasers, Rover, and Goalie alignments in somewhat of a free-lance maneuver.

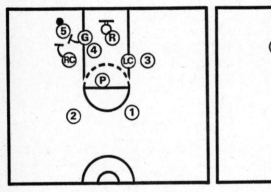

Diagram 3-20

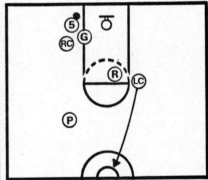

Diagram 3-21

We have found that pressing after a missed shot is an effective tactic, especially as a surprise. Many teams have a definite fullcourt press offense from an out-of-bounds situation with designated people in set spots. Springing this surprise maneuver after a missed field goal attempt frequently upsets the offensive squad's "applecart." For instance, in the example in Diagram 3-20 let us presume that the opponents usually designate their two guards (players 1 and 2) to be in the primary inbounds receiving positions with a forward player (3) as the inbounds passer. Many teams use a similar formation setup. The usually poor ball-handling players, 4 (the other forward) and 5 (the center), are downcourt, usually against a fullcourt press situation. However, when the press is in action after a missed shot attempt, as in the example in Diagrams 3-20 and 3-21, as the center player (5) rebounds he is immediately faced with a doubleup situation with ball-handling responsibilities. He is probably now in an unfamiliar situation and is out of "position." The three normal ball handlers, the two guards (1 and 2) and the inbounds passer (3), are also out of their usual designated press alignments. This may cause immediate confusion and a jumbled situation. Unless a team practices against this type of confrontation they may have a multitude of problems. We have also discovered that by interchanging the positions the players get to know, respect, and understand the responsibilities and functions of the entire press.

THE RETREAT TO THE GOAL

The pressing team must be sure to keep the goal area guarded to avoid the morale defeating layup. Whenever the press is broken, the entire defense only has split seconds in which to avoid getting "burned" by the offense. This is the crisis time for the press. All double-teamers must be drilled to sprint back as quickly as possible to adjust every time a ball or a player defeats a trap.

Many times, just by hustling back into a press, a presser will get a deflected ball or may even knock the ball from an offensive player on his dribble from behind. We instruct the players to burst back to the 12–15 foot scoring area and then build the defense from this position. You must not allow the offense to score a layup! Frequently the offensive team will get by the first lines of a press only to be confronted by a hustling player or players; and the offense, when denied the surefire layup, will often force a hurried shot, thus playing into our press!

On sequence of coverage, cover the goal first, the ball next, and then protect the remaining danger areas near the ball. The player who watches all the action from behind will not help the defense much, and perhaps he can watch better from the bench beside me.

A single note about the double-team. You should trap like you are stalking an animal. You must not make a wild lunge at the ball handler, he must be eased over and slowed down. When the "animal" is about caged or trapped, put the clamp on. We must pressure yet control the dribbler or ball handler.

TYPES OF DROPBACK DEFENSES

The types of dropback defenses we may use off our presses depend of course on our opponent and the situation. For example, we may drop back into our straight Man/Zone defense, a corner or wing trap pressing maneuver, or into various types of man-to-man coverages.

TIPS ON TEACHING THE MAN/ZONE PRESSURE DEFENSE

The following are some tips for teaching the pressure defense:

1. Outline your zone (or man) pressure defense on paper and give each player a copy.
2. Drill your squad well in pressure defense fundamentals.
3. Know the defense backwards and forwards before you try to teach it. Use the chalkboard and diagram the various tactics. A portable board on the floor would be ideal.
4. Walk through the defensive moves on the court.
5. Then go one-half speed on the court with no offense.
6. Now go full speed and add offense.
7. Develop an offense that is designed to attack the known trouble areas and then use it against your presses in practice. As soon as a defensive mistake is made or the offense scores a basket, you should immediately stop the scrimmage. Now retrace each step until you find out why the defense broke down.

THE USE OF "SITUATION CARDS" AS AN AID

Use any number of situations that you can with your pressure defenses. We use around 20. They are written on 3″ x 5″ cards as in Diagrams 3-22 and 3-23. The cards are shuffled and given to each member of the team. Each player is given a few seconds to explain (with the coach's assistance) the situation and the probable remedy. The manager will then put the situation on the scoreboard. We have found that the "situation cards" tend to give our squad confidence and high morale in panic situations.

SCORE: We are down by 5 points

TIME ON CLOCK: 3 minutes remaining

Suggestions: You are in 75 Green. The opposition is playing deliberately. You may have to intentionally foul. The dropback defense is a pressing zone. You must know the bonus situation.

Diagram 3-22

SCORE: We are down by 1 point

TIME ON CLOCK: 1 minute remaining and a defensive jumpball

Suggestions: If you lose possession you are in Orange 75. The dropback defense is tight man-to-man. You must know the bonus situation.

Diagram 3-23

SCOUTING AS AN AID TO THE PRESSING GAME

We believe in extensive scouting. To make our press successful we use the following form which has proven to be a great aid in developing our "press game strategy." (See Diagram 3-24.) We prepare our game plan and practice schedule from the information taken from the scouting report.

An important point is that there is nothing a coach would rather do than scout a future opponent himself. Usually, however, the coach's schedule prevents this and the job falls to an assistant coach or a friend. This means the scout must know what the coach wants, and do the job right.

Team scouted_____vs._____ at _____
Versus what type presses?_____
_____

I. THE TRIGGERMAN (Inbounds Passer) _____
    Does he favor one side of the basket?_____
    How far back from the endline does he stand?_____
    What is his height?_____
    Is he right- or left-handed?_____
    How fast does he get ball before he makes the pass in?_____
    Does he stay in one spot or does he move?_____
    Will he throw the bomb?_____
    Once he gets ball inbounds, does he sprint down the
        floor or is he a safety outlet?_____
    Will they use two men out-of-bounds?_____
    Does he delay until the offense is set? _____
    Do they use a screen to keep pressure off him?_____
    After the pass inbounds, do they screen for him? _____
    Can he be bothered? _____

II. THE NEAR INBOUNDS MEN _____
    Will they cross or screen for each other?_____
    Will they fake deep and burst for basket?_____
    Who is weakest ball handler?_____ best?_____
    Where do they position themselves initially?_____
    On pass, what is usual next move?_____
    What are their heights?_____
    Are they right-or left-handed?_____
    Will they look to throw the bomb?_____
    Will either or both step out-of-bounds to receive pass
        from the triggerman? _____
    Do they look to the middle?_____ or go sideline?_____
        or reverse ball?_____
    Can they be bothered?_____

III. THE FAR INBOUNDS MEN _____
    Do they play strong or weakside?_____
    What are their heights?_____
    Will they cut to middle to help?_____
    If they receive pass do they pass?_____ dribble?_____
        reverse ball?_____ turn and pass downcourt?_____

Diagram 3-24

Will they screen to free a player?_____
Who is the best ball handler?_____ weakest?_____
Can they be bothered?_____

IV. TEAM—GENERAL CHARACTERISTICS
   Will they try to "run" for the score and beat
      the press down the floor?_____
   Will they beat the press past the ten-second line and
      then set up the offense?_____
   What kind of shot do they look for? layup?_____ jumper?_____
   Do they take hurried shots?_____
   Do they fast break down middle?_____ sideline?_____
   Do they follow a pattern?_____ free-lance?_____
   Do they have a *different* set pattern when being
      pressed after a miss?_____
   A *different* pattern when ball is on sideline?_____
   How many players do they have in backcourt?_____
   When should we press them: after a made field goal?_____
      after a made free throw?_____ after a miss?_____
      on sideline?_____
   Are they in condition?_____
   Are they poised or easily rattled?_____

   ADDITIONAL COMMENTS:
   RECOMMENDATIONS_____
   _____
   _____
   _____

   FOLLOW-UP (After Game)_____
   _____
   _____
   _____

VIDEO TAPE EVALUATION:

Diagram 3-24 (continued)

PRESSURE DEFENSE DRILLS

   The pressure defense drills listed in this section have been
tested and proven over a number of seasons and have aided greatly
in making the pressure defense a success.

1. FOUR ON TWO FULLCOURT
   Player 1 dribbles and is trapped by X1 and X2. Player 2
   comes over to get pass from 1 when 1 becomes trapped.
   Two then drives left and is trapped by X3 and X4. Player 1
   then comes back (X1 and X2 allow him to get ball) and is
   double-teamed again by X1 and X2. Two traps to each
   side end the drill and all six players fall back into line and
   six more players take the court. When the players take the
   court again they exchange positions. (See Diagram 3-25.)

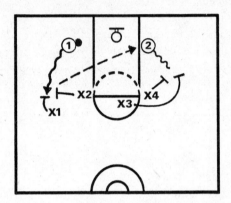

Diagram 3-25

2. COMPETITION DRILL
   Team A takes the ball down the floor and Team B presses.
   When Team A makes a violation or scores, Team B gets
   the ball and goes against A's defense. If the defensive
   team steals the ball, they still get the ball on offense in
   their regular turn, regardless of whether they score or not.
   The winner is the first team to score 21 points. Points are
   scored in the following manner:

   1 point—basket
   1 point—free throw (every foul and one-and-one)
   1 point—steal
   1 point—each violation

3. RUN OFFENSE AND THEN PRESS
   You can work on your offensive timing while pressing in
   this drill. Team A runs their offense against Team B's

defense at halfcourt. As soon as A makes a score or loses possession they use a pressure defense on B. The same scoring as in Drill 2 may be used.

4. SOFTBALL
    You play a 7 "inning" softball game. Team A takes the ball out against Team B and tries to score. If A scores they are credited with 1 run. If B gets the ball it is an out, and after 3 outs B gains possession. As an alternate, in 2 out situations a score nullifies the outs.

5. TWO OFFENSIVE VERSUS THREE DEFENSIVE
    This drill also affords work on offense as well as defense. Two offensive players move the ball the length of the court (only one player can dribble). The two defensive players double-team the dribbler while the third defensive player guards the other offensive player closely. If the defense gets the ball, the offense must do 20 pushups. The players then exchange lines.

6. ANTICIPATION DRILL
    Team A lines up in their press formation. There are four offensive players on the court and the fifth player (or coach) attempts to pass to them. This is a great teacher for anticipation.

7. THREE ON TWO TRAP DRILL
    See Diagram 3-26. Players 1 and 2 advance the ball upcourt against three defensive players (X1, X2, and X3). The offensive players cannot cross the center line until the ball does.

8. TWO ON ONE DEEP PASS DRILL
    See Diagram 3-27. Dribbler 1 can pass down the floor anytime, but player 2 must stay deep down the court. If player 1 gets by the defense (X1 and X2) then the back defensive player (X3) plays 1 versus 2 defense.

The fullcourt press has been good to us, pulling many a game out of the jaws of defeat. I can well recall trailing by 6 points with 20 seconds remaining in a conference championship game, and winning the game in regulation time by two points because of the press.

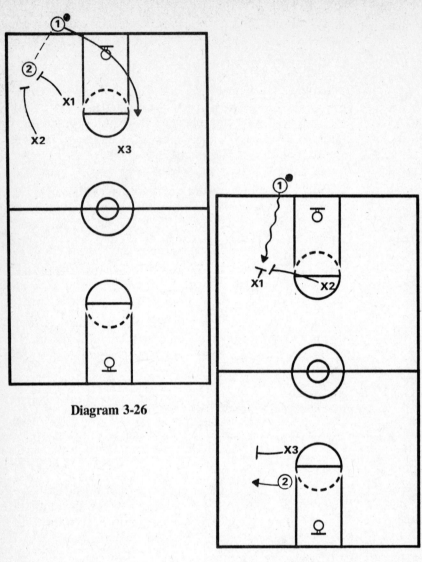

Diagram 3-26

Diagram 3-27

4

SUPPLEMENTING
THE PRESSURE DEFENSES

The pressure defenses illustrated in this chapter are supplementary presses used as a change of pace. As previously stated, we like to do the unorthodox to make the opponent play a little differently. For instance if the opponent is attacking pressure by going to the middle of the floor and we are using the Green 100 press, we may change to the orange 75 (2-1-1-1 press) which forces the ball down the sideline. We like to use pressure formations that are not used or seen much by the opponents.

We may also alternate positions on the floor, one time attacking with a fullcourt (100), another time with a three-quarter court (75), or with a halfcourt (50) or quartercourt (25) trapping formations. In this chapter we will depict a few pressure defenses that you can use that are a little unorthodox in alignment and are not used by many teams.

BIG MAN BLUE 100

The Pincher, who in this press is usually the quickest big man, tries to get to the man out-of-bounds right away to stall the offense and give his teammates time to get to their positions. The Pincher should defend in the same manner as he does on the Green 100.

If the pass inbounds is allowed to be made uncontested, it should be in front of the Left and Right Chasers. If no opponent is in front of his initial position, the Chaser should drop back toward the nearest offensive player on his side or into the middle of the backcourt to prevent a pass over the Pincher and the other Chaser.

The Right Chaser and Left Chaser take positions at about three feet from the free throw line extended and do not cross an imaginary line down the center of the court. (See Diagram 4-1.) The main responsibility of both Chasers is to force the man with the ball into a double-team with the Pincher. Usually, the Left Chaser is another big man while the Right Chaser can be a guard. Of course the Chaser alignment would change if the ball were taken out consistently on the left side of the floor. The Chasers usually allow the first pass inbounds, but may try to force the opponents as close to the endline as possible.

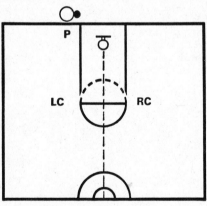

Diagram 4-1

The Rover overplays to the side of the ball in the middle of the court, almost in an imaginary direct line with the Pincher. This is a very key position and is generally played by our fastest and most agile guard. The man playing the Rover in this press must have good lateral movement and excellent anticipatory qualities. The Rover lines up about three feet in front of the midcourt circle. He must prevent a pass coming directly to the middle of the court from out-of-bounds. He will go only as far as the top of the key extended, as in Diagram 4-2, to prevent the pass.

The Goalie must protect the scoring area. He is usually the small forward in the press and must stop the layup. The Goalie never leaves this area near the goal unless he is sure of an interception. He should be intelligent and be able to diagnose passes and defend against 2 on 1, 3 on 1, 4 on 1, and sometimes 5 on 1. The Goalie lines up at about the top of the key area initially.

Diagram 4-3 shows that as the ball comes in from offensive player 1 to 2, the Pincher traps to the side of the ball, not allowing 2

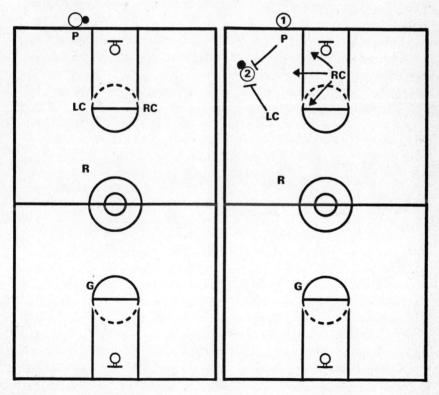

Diagram 4-2   **Diagram 4-3**

to come back on the baseline side. The Pincher applies pressure to the man out-of-bounds, his arms up in a windmilling fashion while jumping up and down. By keeping his hands up, he can deflect and even steal many passes which can be turned into easy baskets. If the Pincher does a good job he eliminates the long bomb pass to the midcourt area or deeper.

The Left Chaser comes up to double-team with the Pincher and does not allow 2 to come down the sideline. Both players keep their hands up, trying to force a lob pass. The Left Chaser should overplay 2 with his inside leg lined up with 2's crotch. The Pincher and Left Chaser form a "V," with the man they are double-teaming in the trough of the "V." The Right Chaser, who does not have the ball on his side (imaginary line), moves into an intercepting position. The Right Chaser is also responsible for covering 1 if 2 returns a pass. The Pincher would then come over to doubleup with the Right Chaser on 1.

The Rover plays the middle of the court directly in line with the ball. The Rover always plays a man in his zone area if he is on the side of the ball. If 2 would pass the ball to 4, the Rover would be responsible for stopping the ball and he would double-team with the Left Chaser. In this double-team, as in all double-teams in this book, the trappers would use the "V" technique as described in the previous paragraph.

Once the ball is past a defensive player's position he must turn and sprint in a straight line to the goal area, in direct proportion to the speed of the ball until he is back and ahead of it.

The Goalie plays at the top of the key and defends any man in this area. As soon as the ball reaches the midcourt area, he drops back to the dotted circle on the free throw lane. If the Goalie is sure he can intercept the pass he may come up high.

As indicated in Diagram 4-4, if 2 would dribble across on the baseline the Pincher would slide across with him and trap with the Right Chaser. The Left Chaser would float in the middle going as far as the imaginary line.

In the example in Diagram 4-5, 2 beats the Left Chaser and dribbles down the sideline and must be stopped by the Rover. The Right Chaser and Pincher must burst downcourt to help out. If possible, the Left Chaser should drop to attempt a double-team with the Rover.

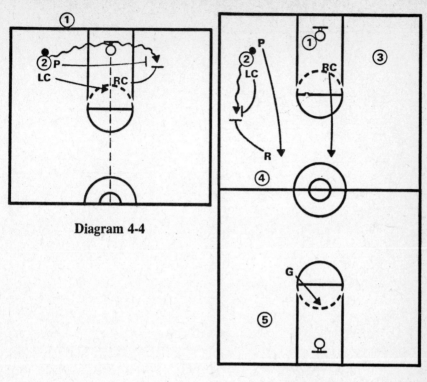

Diagram 4-4

Diagram 4-5

As in Diagram 4-6, if the Pincher would do a poor job and allow a direct pass from 1 to 4, the Rover would come up to stop 4 and the Pincher bursts to double-team with the Rover. The two Chasers float with their men in their area, coming back in a straight line until they are ahead of the ball and at the same time attempting to cover the passing lanes.

In Diagram 4-7 an adjustment can be made for teams who play all five offensive men in the frontcourt. The Goalie can "cheat" up and take the weakside man while the Rover takes the strongside as usual. It should be pointed out that at any time with the Big Man Blue 100 press, you can revert to the "freeze em" press as a change of pace. All players try to shut off their man for five seconds to force a 5-second out-of-bounds violation.

In Diagram 4-8 a sideline out-of-bounds situation is illustrated with the alignment of the defensive players.

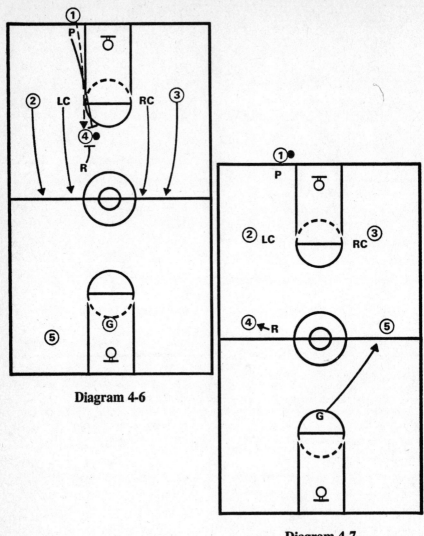

Diagram 4-6

Diagram 4-7

RETREAT TO THE GOAL DRILL

This is one of the drills used to practice retreating to a goal line defense when your pressure defense has been broken. You should set up in one of your fullcourt, three-quarter court, or halfcourt pressure defenses, such as the Green 75 described in Chapter 3.

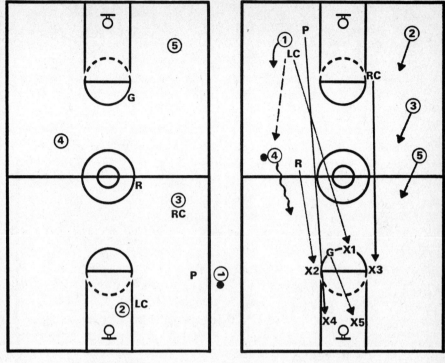

Diagram 4-8   **Diagram 4-9**

You set up five offensive men and place them in position as in Diagram 4-9. The purpose of the drill is to have the defense release and retreat to the goal and be in the Man/Zone defense (detailed in Chapter 2) within four seconds after the ball leaves the passer's hand. The passer moves to different areas on the court.

In Diagram 4-9, as 1 passes to 4 the Rover must allow the pass to be completed. The five defensive players must sprint to the goal and the five offensive players also "run" to the basket in an effort to beat the defense. Use the scoreboard clock or a stopwatch (preferred) to time the four seconds and have a manager or assistant coach blow a whistle to have all the players "freeze" in their tracks on the court. You can readily tell who is not getting the job done retreat-wise. The defense must be back in the Man/Zone in proper stance within four seconds.

The Pincher in this example has the most territory to cover

since he must drop to a deep post-position. The Left Chaser drops to the point, the Right Chaser and Rover to the wings, and the Goalie to a deep post-position.

Diagram 4-10 depicts the retreat from a fullcourt pressure defense (Big Man Blue 100) to the Man/Zone. This must also be done in four seconds. Again the Pincher has the responsibility of dropping all the way to the deep post-position. If this is too difficult for the Pincher, you can adjust by allowing him to drop to the wing or point position and having the Rover drop to a deep post-position if feasible. Again all five players must be back in the Man/Zone in proper defensive position within four seconds.

Diagram 4-11 illustrates the same drill from a halfcourt (Blue 50) pressure defense. Here the defense must retreat within two seconds to the Man/Zone. Again, the Left Chaser must allow the pass to be completed. As soon as the pass leaves 2's hand, everyone retreats on defense and the five offensive players sprint to the basket in fast-break fashion. An adjustment can again be made by allowing the Rover to fill a deep post-position and having the Pincher take the wing or point slots. All five defensive men must be in position in two seconds.

The very first objective is to get the squad back in time to defend the goal. All five players have to get downfloor immediately after ball possession is lost. In sequence of importance, you must cover the goal first, the ball second, and the remaining critical area third.

ORANGE 75

In my years of coaching I have not seen another team use the Orange 75 (or 2-1-1-1) pressure defense. It forces the opponent to do things a little differently. If the opposition has consistently gone to the middle of one of the other pressure defenses, you might switch to the Orange 75 which forces the ball down the sideline.

As illustrated in Diagram 4-12, the initial starting alignment will have the two Chasers a step in the lane at approximately the free throw line extended. The Pincher plays about four feet in front of the center circle and the Rover is about four feet behind it. The Goalie starts at the opposite free throw circle. The Rover and the Pincher must be good anticipators and able to pick off the long

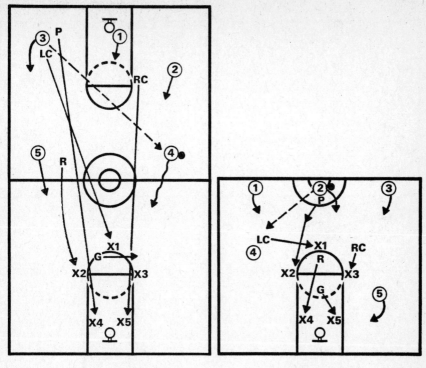

Diagram 4-10   Diagram 4-11

bomb pass. The Goalie only comes up when he absolutely has an interception. In this alignment the Chasers will usually be your guards, the Pincher and Rover your forwards, and the Goalie your center.

As shown in Diagram 4-12, the Left Chaser comes up with hands up on 2 as 2 receives the ball, and does not allow 2 to come to the middle or come back on the baseline side. The Right Chaser also comes over with hands up to discourage 2 from coming to the baseline side and to cover 1 if 2 attempts a backpass. The objective is to make 2 dribble down the sideline. The Pincher should "wait" until he is sure 2 is going to dribble down the sideline, and then he attacks in a good defensive stance with hands up and he double-teams with the Left Chaser. The Rover and Goalie both move to the left looking to pick off a pass. The Right Chaser drops and floats in the middle also looking to pick off a possible pass.

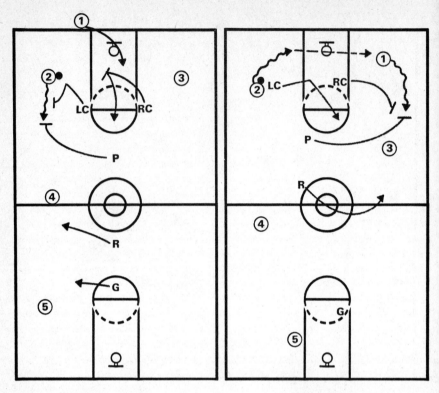

Diagram 4-12   **Diagram 4-13**

In Diagram 4-13, if 2 does not go down the sideline and evades the Left Chaser and then passes to 1 who dribbles down the right sideline, the Left Chaser would drop and float to the middle and the Right Chaser would herd 1 down the sideline and then into a double-team. The Pincher "waits" until he is sure 1 is going to dribble and then he attacks and double-teams with the Right Chaser. If 1 evades the trap it would be the Rover's responsibility to stop the dribbler and the Rover would trap with the Pincher. The Chasers would sprint to the basket while looking for a possible deflection or steal. The Goalie would cheat slightly to the right side of the free throw lane.

As depicted in Diagram 4-14, if 1 completes a pass directly to 4 the Rover must come up to stop 4 and the Pincher joins him in a double-team. The Chasers break to the opposite end of the court

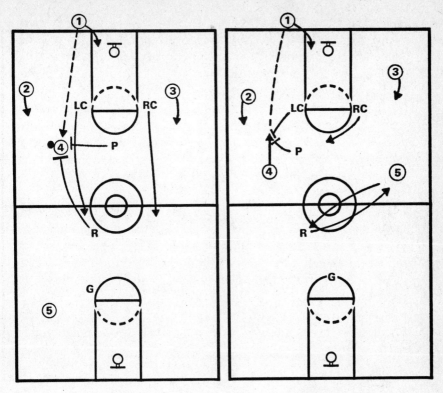

Diagram 4-14   **Diagram 4-15**

looking for a possible steal or deflection on their way to help the Goalie. The Goalie has moved over slightly to the left side of the free throw lane.

In Diagram 4-15, if 1 attempts a pass over the defense by placing two men at the timeline the defense should adjust. The Pincher would move over a step or two and the Rover would move up as illustrated. If the pass would come in to 4, 4 would be trapped by the Left Chaser and the Pincher with the Right Chaser floating. The Rover would sag to the middle and the Goalie would stay at home.

HAWK OR BLUE 50

Another pressure defense that is effective is a halfcourt maneuver called the "Hawk" or "Blue 50." The Green 75 defense detailed in Chapter 3 had the element of an unorthodox rotation among the five defensive players. We have not seen this type of rotation by any other team in our years of coaching. The Orange 75 mentioned in the last section also had an unusual alignment that we have never encountered in an opponent.

The Hawk or Blue 50 pressure defense has still another unique trait. While this actual formation has been used against our teams many times, the Blue 50 has the unorthodox feature of not trapping in the corner which seems to throw an opponent off. Also, we generally use our big man at the Pincher position at the timeline which is somewhat unique.

The Blue 50 was directly responsible for an upset victory over one of our rivals. We trailed by five points late in the fourth quarter and switched to the Blue 50. Our aggressive Pincher forced our opponent to commit two traveling violations and to make two bad passes in his next four ball possessions. As a result, we tallied four baskets and hung on for a narrow two-point victory.

The initial starting positions are depicted in Diagram 4-16. The Pincher lines up on the timeline in the middle of the center circle.

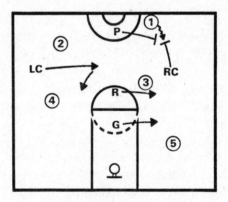

Diagram 4-16

The Left Chaser and Right Chaser get in position at approximately the 28-foot hash mark extended. The Rover positions himself at approximately the top of the free throw circle twenty feet from the basket. The Goalie plays in the lane between the dotted circle and the free throw line. The Pincher should be your big forward or center. The Left Chaser should be a forward and the Right Chaser a guard. Most teams are right-handed and will attack from the left side of the court, so the Right Chaser should be the quicker of the two Chasers because he will have more territory to cover. The Rover should be your quickest guard and should have good court savvy and good anticipatory abilities. The Goalie should be your big forward or center.

Ideally, as in Diagram 4-16, you would want the Pincher to force the dribbler to his weak hand. Most players are right-handed, so you would try and force 1 (in this example) to his left and down the right side of the court. The key to this defense is to never let the offense go to the middle of the floor. When the Pincher forces 1 down the sideline, the Right Chaser holds his position until he sees 1 dribbling down the sideline and then he charges hard, while still under good defensive balance, and forms a trap on 1 with the Pincher. The Right Chaser's and Pincher's hands must be held high to force a lob pass. The Left Chaser sags to the middle and the Rover goes towards the outside of the free throw lane, adjusting his position with the offensive man in his area. The Goalie cheats slightly to about a step outside the foul lane. On a pass to the corner, if the Goalie is absolutely sure of intercepting it he may leave his position. Otherwise he stays in an area surrounding the goal.

The two double-teamers (Right Chaser and Pincher in Diagram 4-16) must not allow the offensive player (1 in this example) to split them in any way. The Left Chaser, or the weakside wingman, plays his position according to where the offense places their men. If the offense puts a man in the free throw circle area and a man in the backcourt area, the Left Chaser would take the closest man to the basket.

In Diagram 4-17, if 1 passes to 3 in the wing area, the Rover picks up 3 and is joined in a double-team by the Right Chaser. The Pincher sags about four feet outside the free throw lane. The Left Chaser sags to the free throw line extended and the Goalie retreats near the basket.

In Diagram 4-18, on a pass to the corner we never trap in this area with this particular pressure defense. However if the Goalie sees that the Rover cannot get to the corner in time, he picks up 5 until the Rover can get there. When the Rover arrives on the ball the

Goalie quickly retreats to the foul lane. The weakside wing (Left Chaser), the Right Chaser, and the Pincher all sink to the basket as depicted in 4-18.

As in Diagram 4-19, if 1 passes the ball to 3 in the middle of the defense the Rover immediately comes up to stop the ball. The Pincher immediately collapses to the ball and double-teams with the Rover. The two Chasers sag deep to the basket to help the Goalie.

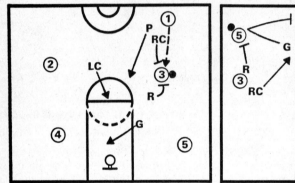
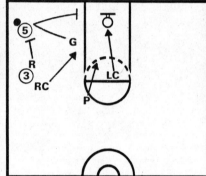

Diagram 4-17   **Diagram 4-18**

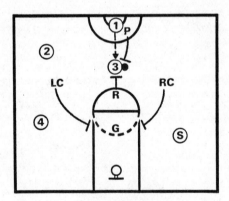

Diagram 4-19

THE 1-1-3 PRESSURE DEFENSE

As illustrated in Diagram 4-20, the 1-1-3 pressure defense, or the Black 50, is another unorthodox alignment that you can throw at the opponent to frustrate him. This is again a defense that we have not seen used by any opponent.

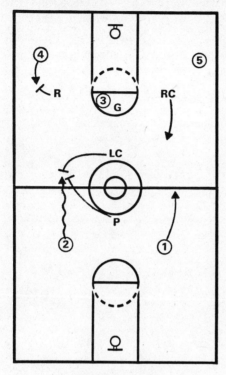

Diagram 4-20

The starting position has the Pincher about a foot in front of the center circle in the midcourt area. The Left Chaser lines up at the tip of the free throw circle in backcourt. The Rover, Goalie, and Right Chaser start at the free throw line extended. The Pincher and Left Chaser should be your guards, the Rover and Right Chaser your forwards, and the Goalie your center.

The Pincher should try to get offensive player 2 to use his weak hand (force right-hander left, left-hander right) and force dribbler 2 into a double-team with the Left Chaser. A coaching tip here would be that the closer the offensive man is trapped to the timeline the more effective the press. Occasionally, an offensive player will dribble or fumble the ball across the timeline for an over and back violation if great pressure is *suddenly* put on. The weakside man, the Right Chaser, will come up high and place himself between the offensive man with the ball and player 1. The Rover will guard anyone above the free throw line extended man-to-man and over-play him if possible. In Diagram 4-20 the Rover is overplaying 4. The Goalie will protect the highpost but will not cover higher than the top of the key area.

In Diagram 4-21, 2 makes a cross court pass to 5 and the Goalie, who sinks to the baseline first, goes out to the corner to trap with the Right Chaser. The Pincher sags to the right side of the highpost area. The Left Chaser sprints to a fronting position directly under the basket. A coaching rule here is that the Goalie does not leave to go to the corner until the Left Chaser is arriving to fill his spot. The Rover sags to a weakside slot.

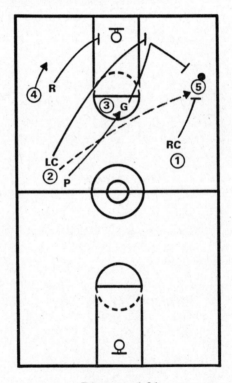

Diagram 4-21

Diagram 4-22 illustrates the move if the pass goes to the middle of the 1-1-3 pressure defense. In the example, 1 passes to 3. The Right Chaser would quickly move over and take 3 while the Goalie would immediately drop to the goal area, being aware of the possibility that 5 and 4 might break to the basket. The Rover and Left Chaser would immediately drop to the basket to help the Goalie. The Pincher would collapse and attempt to doubleup on 3 with the Right Chaser.

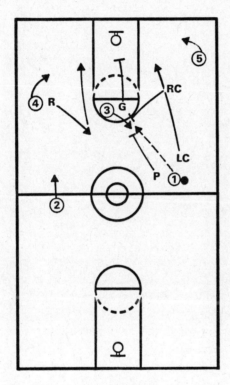

Diagram 4-22

5

USING VARIATIONS WITH
THE MAN/ZONE DEFENSE

If you are not using a pressure defense and the Man/Zone defense is going well, you should generally stay with the basic, normal slides of the Man/Zone. However, if the opposition is successful in its offensive attack or your offense is sluggish or ineffective, you might switch to one or several of the Man/Zone variations that will be detailed in this chapter. You can also use variations of the Man/Zone as a change of pace during various intervals of a game to "feel out" your opponent.

Opposing scouts have told me they have trouble deciphering the Man/Zone as it seems that it does not follow any standard slide movements. This is somewhat true due to the numerous variations applied to the Man/Zone which make practicing against it by the opponent nearly impossible. Some of the variations you may wish to use are the wing and post traps; special kinds of coverage when the ball gets inside the dangerous pivot area; going against a cardinal

rule of defense by ''forcing'' the offensive player to drive the
baseline; covering the corner with a wingman (X2 or X3) in certain
situations; fronting the lowpost with a weakside wingman or the
point player (X1); changing to certain combination defenses when
necessary; and switching to a different zone-type alignment and/or
man-to-man formation in spot situations. These Man/Zone variations will be presented in this chapter.

DOUBLE-TEAMING WITH THE POST AND WING TRAPS

Recently we played an important semi-final tourney game and
the first quarter saw our offense garner zero baskets in thirteen field
goal attempts! Ordinarily you would expect to be ''blown out'' of
the ball game in such a situation. Luckily the Man/Zone was holding
its own, allowing only four baskets in sixteen field goal attempts.
We had managed three free throws but trailed at the quarter 10 to 3.
A switch to the post trap helped to ignite our offense by causing
numerous turnovers by the opposition and we moved to a 34–18 half
time lead. The opponent adjusted in the second half and played
evenly with us, but the second quarter spurt with a slight Man/Zone
variation had proved to be the difference in a 16 point victory.

POST TRAP (Green 25): In Diagram 5-1, on a pass to the right
corner X5 and X2 break to the corner and trap in a wide stance with
hands held high, using similar trap procedures as described in Chapter 3. The key is to have X5 and X2 arrive on offensive player 3 as
simultaneously as possible, with hands high to force a lob pass. X4

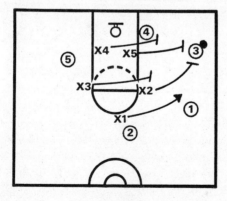

Diagram 5-1

fills X5's spot and fronts anyone in the right lowpost area. X4 would also be responsible for a long pass over his head to the weakside area, especially in the left lowpost area which is left totally un-guarded as X3 moves over to front anyone in the high lane area on the right side. X1 splits between the corner and 1, looking for a possible pick-off of a backpass from 3. The completed post trap alignment is illustrated in Diagram 5-2.

Another variation of a post trap is depicted in Diagram 5-3. X4 is caught behind offensive player 4, as 4 receives the pass from 3. Remember our rule to always front in this area if possible. In this example, X4 was unable to front. This situation signals X5 to quickly move in and double-team with X4. X5 and X4 use all the trapping techniques described in Chapter 3. X2 and X1 are espe-cially alert for a possible interception of a backpass by 4. X3 is responsible on the weakside. If 4 passes back out to corner man 3 as described in 5-4, an unorthodox maneuver is used as X5 stays in his fronting position on 4 and X4 breaks out to cover corner player 3. X1, X2, and X3 remain in position looking to help out if necessary.

Another adjustment to the post trap is depicted in Diagram 5-5. X5 covers the ball and X4 fronts in the right lowpost area. X3 fills in the high lane area and X1 fronts anyone in the high post area on the right side, looking for a possible deep backcourt pass. The major difference in this Man/Zone variation is that X2, instead of trapping with X5 in the corner, drops off and plays the passing lane. Many times, an offensive player "caught" in the corner in this situation, especially without a dribble, is called for a 5-second held ball viola-tion.

WING TRAP (Green 25A): Diagram 5-6 illustrates a trap when the ball is at the rightwing position. As offensive player 1 passes to 2, X1 and X2 apply all trapping rules and must arrive as simultane-ously as possible. X5 cheats over slightly towards the corner, ready to pick off a lob pass to 4. If X1 and X2 have their hands held high, it should be a high lob pass. X3 moves over to the highpost area and is ready to pick-off a pass in this area and also steal a possible backpass to 1. Another key here is X4, who comes as high as the dotted circle in the free throw lane to steal a possible pass in this area, but who is also responsible for a possible weakside pass over his head.

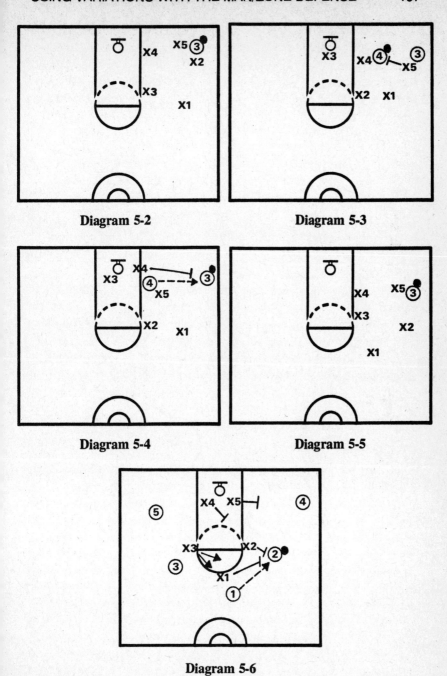

Diagram 5-2

Diagram 5-3

Diagram 5-4

Diagram 5-5

Diagram 5-6

Diagram 5-7 illustrates a variation of the wing trap when offensive player 2 dribbles to the right corner. X2 goes with 2 and X5 fronts anyone in the right lowpost area. X4, who is normally one of the best rebounders, stays at home in the weakside area. X3 moves to the middle of the lane in the middle highpost area. X1 fronts anyone in the high post area.

Diagram 5-8 shows another variation of the Man/Zone wing trap when 1 makes a direct pass (or skip pass, skipping offensive player 2) to 5 in the right corner. Normally, in the basic Man/Zone slides, X5 would cover this pass. If you have a defensive player in the wing position (X2 or X3) with speed and good anticipatory abilities, you can make the moves as in Diagram 5-8 with X2 sliding to the right corner. Again X5 fronts in the right lowpost area and X4 stays at home. X1 fronts in the highpost area and X3 moves over to the middle of the lane.

In Diagram 5-9, another maneuver off of the Man/Zone is shown as 5 (in the right corner) attempts to dribble out to the rightwing area. X5 covers 5 and comes out with him until rightwing defensive player X2 sags and picks him up. X5 then immediately drops to a lowpost fronting position on the right side replacing X4. X4 then retreats to the weakside replacing X3. X3 moves to the middle of the lane. X1 takes a low highpost position.

SPECIAL PIVOT COVERAGES

A normal Man/Zone pivot coverage is described in Chapter 1. In this section we will describe "special" pivot coverages which are available in "special" situations. In Diagram 5-10 as offensive player 1 passes to 3 from the left side, X2 picks him up and X1 quickly collapses to the ball using the collapsing techniques described in Chapter 1. If the ball would come in from any point on the right side, X3 would cover. Thus, either wingman X2 or X3, depending on the position of the passer, covers between the ball and the basket. X3 sags slightly, while X4 and X5 keep their normal positions.

Diagram 5-11 shows another special pivot coverage adjustment when the ball is passed inside. In this example X4 has come up from his normal position on the back left side and is trapping with X1 as usual. X1 has collapsed off offensive player 2, who made the

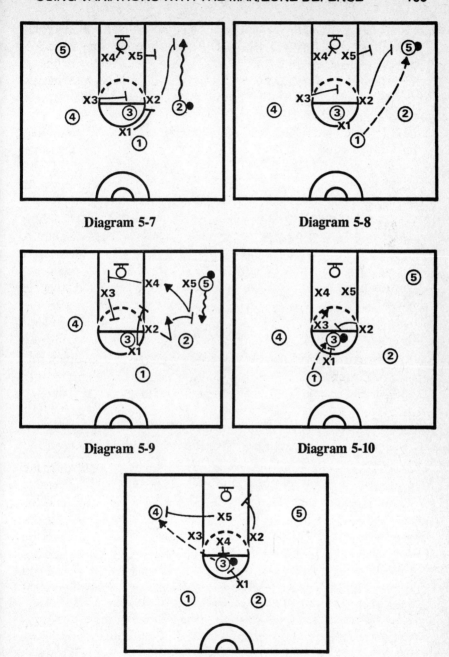

Diagram 5-7

Diagram 5-8

Diagram 5-9

Diagram 5-10

Diagram 5-11

original pass to 3. Also, X3 and X2 have collapsed to the basket and X5 has dropped directly behind X4. X5 has moved over from the right side as normal.

The unorthodox adjustment comes when 3 drops a pass to 4 as illustrated in Diagram 5-11. X5 now takes X4's normal defensive corner (the left side) in covering 4. X4 sinks low and replaces X5 and X4 now assumes X5's responsibilities. X1 X2, and X3 adjust to their normal ball in the corner slides.

Diagram 5-12 depicts still another "surprise" adjustment if you are facing a team having trouble recognizing your defense. You simply adjust to a man-to-man defense. If your opponents don't become aware of this, they will probably attack with their zone offense against your present man-to-man defense. The offense may think you are in the regular Man/Zone or possibly a 2-1-2 zone. In Diagram 5-12, X1 takes guard 2, X3 covers guard 1, X5 slides forward to take center 3, X2 drops to take forward 5, and X4 covers forward 4.

BIG MAN ZORRO

This is a special Man/Zone maneuver that may throw the opposition's offense off stride. It is nicknamed the "Big Man Zorro" and is simply an adjustment made by moving one or both of your tall post players (usually X4 and X5) to the wing and/or occasionally the point defensive positions.

Possibly the best example of the Big man Zorro in action was a few years ago when we played for the conference championship against an opponent who had a prolific scorer averaging over 30 points per game. From the scouting reports it was determined that the opponent's high scorer garnered over 90% of his baskets from the offensive left side of the court with most coming from the leftwing and point areas. The high scorer was tall and was able to riddle most zone-type defenses simply by shooting over them, since in most of these smaller players defend this area of the court.

We placed our players as shown in Diagram 5-13, with a slightly slanted defensive formation to the left side of the floor. The normal post players now manned the leftwing and point positions respectively. The regular point player played the rightwing, the regular leftwing played the left-post, and the normal rightwing played the rightpost. The shaded area in Diagram 5-13 depicts the normal scoring area for the opposition's high scorer. The result was the high scorer forcing several shots over the "wall" on the left side, and this unusual defense seemed to upset him as he was unable to score consistently when he was forced to go to the right side of the floor. He finished with only 12 points, the low score of his brilliant 3-year varsity career, and we had a 10-point upset win and a conference championship.

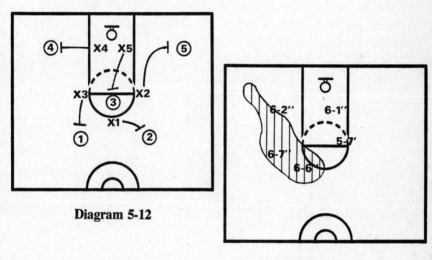

Diagram 5-12

Diagram 5-13

A further variation to the Big Man Zorro can be made if you find, as in this example, the high scorer moving to the offensive rightside and scoring well. You can have the two wings (6'7" and 5'7" in this example) simply exchange places or, as in Diagram 5-13, have the 6'6" pointman and 5'7" rightwing switch as the ball is being reversed. In this way, the whole defensive alignment can overshift to the right.

FORCE BASELINE DEFENSE

One of the oldest defensive axioms in basketball is not to allow a baseline drive by the offense. Most coaches preach that to give up the baseline is a major cardinal sin and they spend endless hours perfecting an adequate baseline defense.

Again the unorthodox is stressed as a major variation in the Man/Zone. Instead of cutting off the baseline, the defensive player invites the offensive player to drive the baseline. Since the offensive player feels he has beaten the defensive man, he drives hard to the basket only to be surprised as he finds himself wedged in a trap.

Diagram 5-14 depicts a pass from offensive player 1 to 5, and as 5 gets the ball he is slightly overplayed by X2 who tries to get 5 to drive the baseline. X2 will play normal defense, not allowing 5 to beat him on the baseline until he reaches an imaginary line even with the backboard (as illustrated in Diagram 5-14). At this position, X2 "allows" 5 to drive by him. Five probably says to himself, "I'm home free for the layup, I can't believe I'm so wide open."

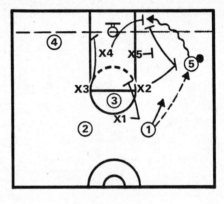

Diagram 5-14

Then, X4 suddenly appears and cuts 5 off. X4 tries to take a defensive charge if possible, but if he is unable to do so he double-teams with X2 at a spot past the imaginary line of the backboard. X3 sinks quickly to the weakside and X5 fronts anyone in the lowpost and looks for a possible interception of a backpass from 5. Five will be in a vulnerable position, because he is suddenly trapped when he thought he had an open layup. Now he can't shoot so he may try to hurry a backpass so he will not be called for a 5-second violation.

The two trappers in this example, X4 and X2, must move quickly and simultaneously, using the basic trapping rules. The same holds true for the other three defensive players. X1 is a key in this defensive alignment as he must cut off all backpasses on the strongside. A long lob pass to the backcourt will not hurt you as the defense will have time to regroup. You will find that after using the "Force Baseline Defense" a few times, the opponent will actually stay away from any ball movement to the corner. You have now taken away a large amount of the opponent's offense, especially those with zone offense attacks.

If the opposition's baseline attack is eliminated, you have to concentrate your defense in a smaller area. The success of the "Force Baseline Defense" depends on stopping the offensive man between the line of the backboard (imaginary line) and the endline. The reason for this is that it is very difficult to score within 12 feet of the basket when the ball is between the line of the backboard and the endline. In fact, it is nearly impossible, especially under pressure.

In Diagram 5-15 another example of the "Force Baseline Defense" is shown as X5 covers 5 and overplays him slightly, inviting him to drive the baseline. X5 attempts to drive 5 into the area between the imaginary line of the backboard and the endline. At this point X5 traps with X2, who suddenly drops from the highpost area.

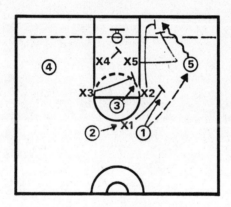

Diagram 5-15

X4 moves over a step or two and stays on the weakside. X3 sinks to the middle of the lane area and looks for a possible steal of a backpass from 5, or X3 will cut off 3 if 3 drops to the lowpost area. X1 slides over quickly and is ready to pick off a possible backpass to 1.

ADJUSTING TO THE COMBINATION DEFENSES

If the Man/Zone defense is having unusual trouble against a certain offense, you may switch to a pressure defense of the quarter, half, three-quarter or full court variety as detailed in Chapters 3 and 4. Or, you may wish to switch to certain variations of the Man/Zone which will be described in this Chapter. You may also want to alter the basic alignment by adjusting to varying units of combination defenses.

The advantages of combination defenses are:

1. Many teams may not have prepared for this unique type of defense.

2. They may completely confuse or frustrate an opponent due to the element of surprise.

The main disadvantages of using combination defenses are:

1. They are definitely weak against good outside shooting teams.

2. They may get your best defensive player in foul trouble.

ADJUSTING TO THE 1-3-1 COMBINATION: As depicted in Diagram 5-16, the basic Man/Zone adjusts to a 1-3-1 zone with X2 moving out to cover offensive player 3. X3 covers 4 and X4 moves up to take 2. X1 takes 1 with the ball and X5 moves directly behind X4 and back about five feet. On a pass of the ball, the defense then shifts to near normal 1-3-1 zone slides.

For example, if the ball were in the rightwing position in the possession of 3 as in Diagram 5-16, X2 would cover 3. X5 fronts in the lowpost area on the right side; X4 jams the lane area fronting if necessary; X3 sags to the weakside; and X1 fronts in the right highpost area.

If the ball were passed to the right corner and was in the possession of 5, X5 would cover him. X4 would front in the right lowpost area; X3 would sag deeper on the weakside; X2 would play in the passing lane or sink to the basket; and X1 would be approximately four feet behind X2 in the lane area.

The same basic slides would take place on the leftside of the floor except when the ball is in the left corner. The middleman (X4) of the 1-3-1 zone would cover this corner with X5 fronting in the left lowpost area.

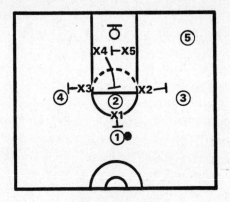

Diagram 5-16

ADJUSTING TO THE 2-1-2 COMBINATION: If a 2-1-2 offense is giving you some trouble, you can adjust from the Man/Zone to a 2-1-2 defensive alignment. As shown in Diagram 5-17, X1 will shift to take the ball with offensive player 1; X2 will cover 3 in the middle; X3 will take the opposite guard (2); X4 and X5 will take their normal positions. The defense then shifts to normal 2-1-2 zone slides.

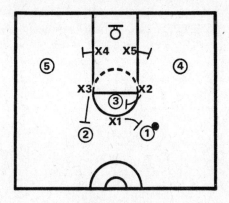

Diagram 5-17

For example, if the ball were passed to 4 in the rightwing area X5 would take 4. X4 would front in the right lowpost and X3 would quickly drop to a deep weakside position. X2 would front at the right free throw line extended and X1 would sag to the middle of the lane.

If the ball were passed to the right corner from the wing, X4 would cover the man in the corner; X3 would sag off the passer; X2 would still be in the right free throw line extended area; and X1 would sag deep to the weakside. The identical slides would take place on the leftside of the floor when the ball is reversed.

ADJUSTING TO THE BOX AND ONE DEFENSE: As illustrated in Diagram 5-18, the Man/Zone may wish to put additional man-to-man pressure on a certain player who is consistently scoring or otherwise successfully hurting the Man/Zone. The Man/Zone might then switch to a Box and One defense as X1 would cover offensive player 4. In this example, 4 is the player you want to apply additional pressure on. The other four defensive players remain in their original positions. Anytime 4 would come in the area of a Man/Zone player other than X1, he would be double-teamed by that player and X1.

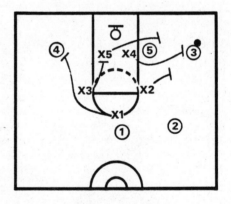

Diagram 5-18

In Diagram 5-18, as offensive player 3 has the ball in the right corner X4 moves out to take 3. X2 would move a couple of steps out of the highpost and X3 would sag in the lane. X5 would front in the right lowpost area and in this case he would front 5. X1 would stay with 4 wherever he goes. If 4 would move to the left highpost area, in the vicinity of X3, as the ball is reversed from 3 to 2 to 1 to 4, 4 would be double-teamed by X3 and X1.

ADJUSTING TO THE DIAMOND AND ONE DEFENSE: If you want to add to your arsenal of combination defenses, you may wish to switch to a variation of the Box and One Defense known as the Diamond and One defense. In Diagram 5-19, as the ball is at the point position X1 plays at the top of the key. X3 and X2 play their normal positions at the free throw line extended. X4 moves over in the middle of the lane directly behind X1, about 13 to 15 feet away. X5 would be on 4 in a one-on-one situation.

In Diagram 5-19, as the ball is passed from 1 to 2, X2 slides out to cover 2. X1 sags in the highpost area and is responsible for covering 3. X4 moves out to a position in the right lowpost area; X3 sags to a position even with the ball and the weakside corner; X5 remains on 4 wherever he goes.

Diagram 5-20 illustrates the situation when the ball is passed to the right corner to 5. X4 slides over to cover 5 and X2 sags back and covers the right highpost area. X3 slides over quickly and covers the right lowpost area. X1 sags to the weakside area and X5 remains on 4 wherever he goes.

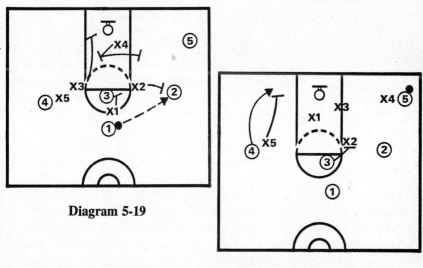

Diagram 5-19

Diagram 5-20

In Diagram 5-21, X5 has continued in his one-on-one coverage on 4 and 4 has gone to the right corner. X4 has sagged back and is responsible for fronting the right lowpost area, in this case offensive player 5. X3 has moved across the lane and is now the weakside defensive man. X2 is in approximately the position as when the ball was at the wing, but he still must be alert to front 3 and be ready to steal a backpass to 2. X1 comes higher in the lane area, approximately 4 or 5 feet behind X2. X1 can also help out on 3 and be ready to intercept a possible cross-court pass to 1. If X5's man should receive the ball inside the post area, he will be double-teamed by the defensive man in the area and X5.

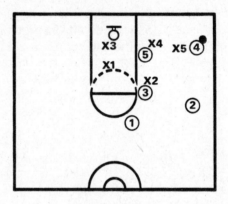

Diagram 5-21

POINTMAN LOW DEFENSE

Another variation of the Man/Zone you can use is to slide your pointman up and down the lane. Your pointman must be quick and aggressive and ideally should have some size to play this variation. This is called the Pointman Low Defense and we have had players ranging from 5'6" to 6'3" in this position.

As illustrated in Diagram 5-22, X2 moves over to take 4 as 4 receives the pass from 1. X1, the pointman and key player in this defense, moves down the lane and is responsible for fronting anyone in the right highpost area. In Diagram 5-22, X1 would be responsible for fronting 3. X3 moves over to the highpost area. X4 and X5 move over slightly, with X5 ready to cover 5 in the corner if the pass goes there from 4.

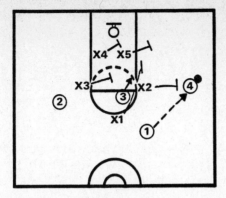

Diagram 5-22

If the ball is reversed from 4 to 1, X3 will temporarily give help to the pointman (X1) until X1 arrives at his original starting position. The wings (X2 and X3) on this defense never have to cover the highpost area since it is covered by X1.

If the ball is passed to 5 in the right corner, as illustrated in Diagram 5-23, X5 will slide out to cover 5. X4 stays in the weakside area and X3 moves over to the right highpost area. X2 sinks back off of 4 to help out if necessary. X1 (the pointman) slides all the way to the right lowpost area and fronts 3 who has also moved down the lane with X1. If the ball is reversed from 5 to 4 to 1 or from 5 to 1 on a skip pass, X3 must help again temporarily in the highpost area until X1 returns to his original starting position.

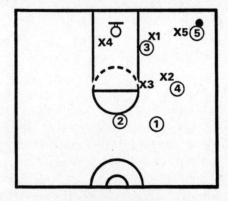

Diagram 5-23

6

CHANGING GAME TEMPO WITH THE MAN/ZONE DEFENSE

The devices detailed in this chapter are tested and proven maneuvers you may desire to use to cause a change of pace, or a change in game tempo, in your game plan. If successful, these confusing methods always seem to frustrate the opposition and somehow injure the morale of the opponent.

UTILIZING THE RELEASE MAN ON A SHOT

An alignment you can use to offset the opponent is the "sleeper." This is set up by releasing to the opposite end of the court a designated player when the opposition makes a field goal attempt. For instance, you should form a triangle (shaded part in Diagram 6-1) with X4, X5, and X3 on the shot from the rightwing area (as usual with the Man/Zone). X1 fronts in the highpost area, but as he sees X5 rebounding he breaks sharply to the sideline. X2 is the sleeper, and he momentarily checks the shooter and then breaks to the other end of the floor. X5 can immediately throw long to X2, pass short to X1, or quickly dribble out and hit X2 long. X2 should buttonhook back to meet the pass if necessary. Once X2 gets the ball, he can either drive hard to the basket, pass to X4 breaking hard down the middle, or pass to X3 who is the trailer on the play.

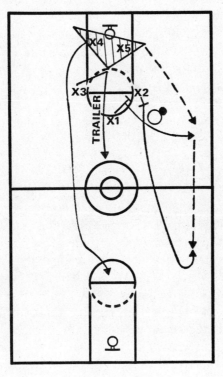

Diagram 6-1

If the shot would come from the leftwing area, X3 would be the release man or "sleeper" and X1 would burst to the left sideline, looking for a quick outlet pass if X4 would be the rebounder. The rebounding triangle would be formed by X4, X5, and X2.

If the field goal attempt would come from the right corner, X2 again would be the release man, X5 would be the short outlet receiver, and the triangle would be formed by X1, X3, and X4.

Let's say for example that on the shot from the right corner, the shot
is rebounded (as often happens) on the weakside by X3. X5, the
short outlet man, must quickly sprint across the lane to the left side
of the court. The release man (X2) on seeing X3 rebounding the ball
on the weakside must also sprint across the floor deep on the left
side, and now strongside, of the court as X3 gathers the ball.

If the shot came from the left corner, X3 would be the release
man, X4 would be the short outlet man, and the triangle would be
formed by X1, X2, and X5.

Another break formation is illustrated in Diagram 6-2. As X4
rebounds, X3 breaks to the strongside sideline. If X3 gets the ball,
he tries to get it to the middle to X1 as he and X2 fill the lanes and
X5 becomes the trailer. If the ball would come out on the right side
and X5 rebounds, X3 would try to pass to X2 by breaking to the
right side line. X2 would try to get the ball to the middle to X1, as
he and X3 fill the lanes and X4 becomes the trailer.

EXPLOITING THE OPPONENT
OFF A DEFENSIVE FREE THROW SITUATION

Another method of exploiting the opponent, especially a larger
but possibly slower one, is to "run" him off a free throw formation.
This is an excellent game tempo alignment, especially against a tall,
pattern-type offensive team. When executed properly, it will force
the opposition to run with the ball which is what such a team
normally dislikes.

Our number one state-ranked team at Elgin, Illinois was at a
disadvantage in the height department in 25 of 28 games that season. Hence we used the formation illustrated in Diagram 6-3 frequently. With this formation you should get 3 on 2 rebound advantages, since you should make the opponent take two players (to
offset your break formation) to at least the midcourt area.

In Diagram 6-3, offensive player 5 makes the free throw and
X5 quickly rebounds, steps out of bounds, and looks for X3 in the
outlet area. X5 must be careful not to break the plane of the endline
as you do not want a quick violation which will require turning the
ball over to the opponent. X3 first blocks out shooter 5 and then
breaks to the side of the court that the ball is rebounded on. In this
example the ball is on the left side. If the free throw is good, as in
Diagram 6-3, X3 will always break out on the left side. X1 fills the

right outside lane. X2 and X1 can (1) fake high and then use a backdoor cut to the goal, (2) X2 can come across and set a screen for X1 and then he can roll to the middle lane, or (3) X2 can set a moving screen on X1 and then break to the middle as in Diagram 6-3.

Diagram 6-4 depicts a missed free throw attempt by offensive player 5 and a subsequent rebound by X4. X3 screens 5, and then noticing X4 rebounding he breaks to the right sideline for a possible outlet pass from X4. X5 fills the left outside lane. In this example X2 and X1 are exercising a fake towards the ball and a backdoor cut. If X3 cannot pass to X1 immediately, he should dribble hard to

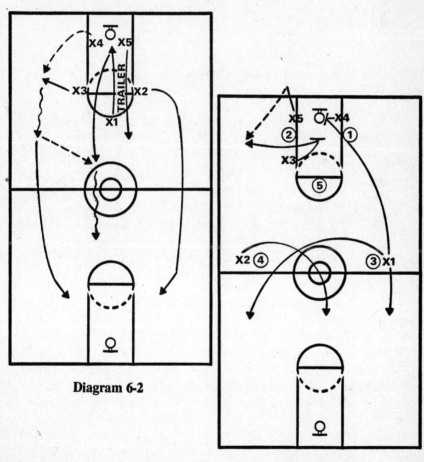

Diagram 6-2

Diagram 6-3

the middle of the court and look for X5, X2, or X1. Another advantage possibly gained is that 5, in his anxiety to rush back on defense or in an attempt to quickly steal an outlet pass, may not concentrate on his free throw and miss.

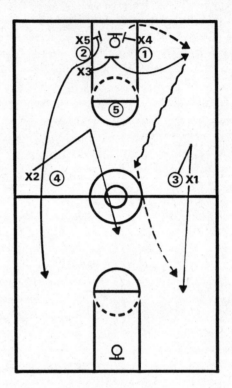

Diagram 6-4

THE VARIOUS USES OF SIGNALS

The use of signals should be investigated thoroughly, carefully scrutinized, and evaluated by every coach. In this section a list of the various ways to signal a defensive change is compiled. These have been tested and used to advantage by the author.

The following is a brief list of the obvious advantages of using signals:

1. You do not have to waste timeouts.

2. By changing your defenses, you may help frustrate the opponent as the element of surprise sets in.

3. The opponent may become so engrossed in your signals and trying to decipher them, that he may not concentrate on the important job at hand—*the game itself!*

If you have in your defensive arsenal various quartercourt, halfcourt, three-quarter court, and fullcourt defenses you better devise a signalling system. There are many ways to signal and some of the most popular that have been used by us are:

1. The coach calls a signal change from the bench.

2. A player calls a signal change from the floor. In both #1 and #2, this becomes very difficult in noisy, crowded gymnasiums. It may be next to impossible to use verbal signals in such cases.

3. The coach makes a hand or finger signal from the bench.

4. A designated player makes a hand or finger signal from the floor.

   An example in #3 and #4 would be that one finger held high in the air would designate a Man/Zone defense; two fingers would mean a fullcourt press of some type, and so on.

5. The coach uses a towel from the bench.

   For example, if the coach holds a towel over his right shoulder you are in halfcourt pressure of some type; over his left shoulder you are in full court pressure; over the knees you are in man-to-man. The coach can also use different color towels to signal a defense, such as a blue towel to indicate you are in the Man/Zone; a red towel for man-to-man; a green towel for a 1-2-2 halfcourt press, etc. In one season we set up so that anytime we would wave a towel when we were in a pressure defense we would immediately drop back to the Man/Zone defense.

6. The coach can use flash cards from the bench.

   The coach can hold up different color cards of varying sizes with each one designating a defense, as the towel colors in #5. Or the coach can hold up a card with a number or letters on it to designate the defense. For

example, in Diagram 6-5 the first two digits would be the
key in a numbering system. Thus, a 12 defense would be
a 1-2-2 quartercourt zone; a 13 defense would be a 1-3-1
quartercourt zone, etc. If you wish to change the quartercourt defense to a pressure type defense you add another
digit, such as 4 to mean a fullcourt pressure; 3 for three-
quarter court pressure; 2 for halfcourt pressure; and 1 for
quartercourt pressure. A 124 defense would be a 1-2-2
fullcourt defense, etc.

Number Signaled	Defensive Alignment	Floor Position
12	1-2-2	Quartercourt
13	1-2-1-1	Quartercourt
122	1-2-2 pressure	Halfcourt
132	1-2-1-1 pressure	Halfcourt
213	2-1-1-1 pressure	Three-quarter court
123	1-2-2 pressure	Three-quarter court
133	1-2-1-1 pressure	Three-quarter court
113	1-1-3 pressure	Halfcourt
124	1-2-2 pressure	Fullcourt
134	1-2-1-1 pressure	Fullcourt

Diagram 6-5

7. The coach can divide the court into sections and give
    each defense a designated color.

    This method is detailed in Chapter 3 and is shown in
    Diagram 3-10. You divide the playing floor into sectors,
    such as 100 for fullcourt; 75 for three-quarter court; 50
    for halfcourt; and 25 for quartercourt. Then you give a
    certain color to each defense.

    For example, when the coach says you are in the
    Green 75 defense you are in a three-quarter pressure de-
    fense of the 1-2-2 formation; Blue 100 defense is a
    fullcourt pressure defense of the 1-2-1-1 formation; an
    Orange 75 defense is a three-quarter court pressure de-
    fense of the 2-1-1-1 formation; a Black 50 is a halfcourt

pressure defense of the 1-1-3 alignment; and a Blue 25 defense would be a pressure defense at quartercourt of the 1-2-1-1 or 1-3-1 variety.

8.   A player can signal by his position on the floor. As illustrated in Diagram 6-6, the Pincher (P) is designated as the signal caller. After you score, if the Pincher lines up on the ball this would alert the remainder of the defense that they are in a full-court pressure defense, for example the Blue 100; if the Pincher lines up at the offensive foul line extended, you are in a three-quarter court pressure defense, for example the Green 75; if the Pincher lines up at midcourt, you are in a halfcourt pressure defense, for example the Black 50; and if the Pincher lines up at the defensive free throw line you are in a quartercourt pressure defense, such as the Green 25.

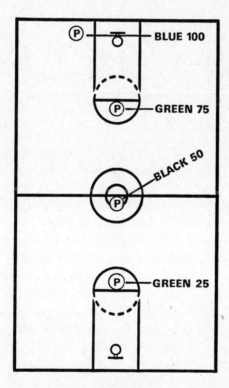

Diagram 6-6

Diagram 6-6 depicts the four basic floor positions of the Pincher.

9.   When shooting a free throw, the players can huddle on the free throw line before the referee hands the ball to your shooter. One designated player can then verbally give the next defense to his teammates.

10.   The coach can raise a magnetic board into the air.

The daring coach can make use of the various kinds of magnetic boards available as coaching aids. These are boards of varying sizes that allow the coach to place his defensive formations on them magnetically. This takes the place of a small chalkboard or diagraming on the floor during timeouts. During one season, we actually signalled the defensive change from the bench by placing the change desired on the magnetic board. Then by raising the board the players could see the change from the floor.

11.   The coach can disguise the signals with positive and negative goemetric symbols.

This approach would be used if a coach wishes to completely camouflage his signals from the bench to his players on the floor. The major value of this signalling is that only you and your players know the symbols and what they mean. An added advantage is that sometimes the opposition may become so engrossed in trying to decipher the signals that they don't concentrate on what they are supposed to be doing. The system is described in Diagram 6-7 and is simply a series of cards with 3-rows of symbols on them.

A series of three geometric symbols (square, triangle, and circle) is arranged in haphazard fashion on a white cardboard sheet approximately 2' x 2' in size. Each symbol is accompanied by its own positive (plus) and negative (minus) sign. Each symbol is a different color as is each positive and negative sign.

The card is divided into thirds and the bottom two-thirds mean absolutely nothing to the viewer. The key is only in the top third of the card. The different colors, designs, and arrangements on each card can be manipulated in any way.

The simple key is as follows:

1. Look in the upper left corner of the card and if a positive sign is there you are in your regular defense—the Man/Zone.

2. If a positive sign is in the upper right corner it means nothing and you should remain in your present defense.

3. If a negative sign appears in the upper left or right corner you are in a pressure defense. If the corresponding symbol is blank you are in a fullcourt press. If it is colored you are in a halfcourt press.

    You can readily see the alternate signs which make each card nearly impossible to decipher. For example, the Man/Zone is shown in Cards 1, 5, and 11. The 1-2-2 fullcourt press in Cards 2 and 12. The 2-1-1-1 fullcourt press in Cards 3 and 7. You can also turn the cards upside down or have any number of cards you desire.

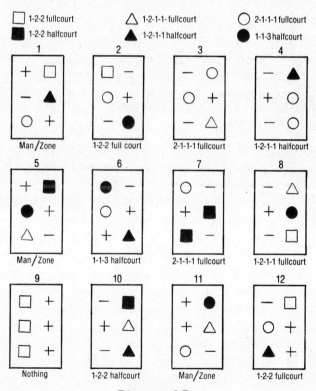

Diagram 6-7

ALTERNATING AND CHANGING DEFENSES
WITH THE MAN/ZONE

The use of alternating or changing defenses has great merit in today's complex game. An alternating defense gives the following advantages to the progressive coach:

1. It upsets a team that has a planned, specific attack for each zone or man-to-man defense.

2. Many teams do not have leaders who readily recognize the changes of various types of defenses.

3. A change helps to prevent staleness and requires all players to be alert.

4. It works excellently as an element of surprise.

5. It helps your team's concentration as all players must be alert.

6. It can change the tempo of the opponent's game.

7. It can give your players a psychological boost by allowing them to play a little differently or in an unorthodox manner.

The disadvantages of using changing or alternating defenses are:

1. A thorough scouting report is usually necessary.

2. Every defensive player must be aware that a change in defensive assignments is being made. You cannot have four players in man-to-man and one player in a zone.

3. Many long hours of practice time are required.

Pointers in Teaching Alternating Defenses:

1. It is recommended that you change from man-to-man to zone or from one type of zone to another zone. It is hard to change from zone to man-to-man in the middle of a pattern.

2. Make sure *all* players know *all* the defenses that you plan to use in detail.

3. Develop a simple signalling system (numbers, colors, etc.) See the previous section in this chapter.

4. Use mimeographed diagrams and distribute them to your players.

5. Use the blackboard for skull session purposes.

6. Go over your scouting reports on the opponent in detail.

7. Use your strongest defense most of the time.

8. You must have extensive practice work on the various alternating or changing defenses.

The following are some of the ways in which you may wish to alternate your defenses. These are automatic defensive changes set up by prior arrangement:

1. Have your two defensive guards alternate positions on the floor in picking up the opponent's guards. One time pick up the opposition fullcourt for a few play sequences; then have them pick up the opposing guards at the far free throw line extended; at the midcourt area; at about the 28-foot hash marks; a few steps from the head of the circle. This tends to throw offensive rhythm out of kilter.

2. You are in the Man/Zone defense. When you make a field goal you change defensively to the Black 50 defense (1-1-3 halfcourt pressure). When you miss a field goal attempt you are back in the Man/Zone.

3. When the opponent comes down on offense and makes a pass to the defensive leftwing area you are in the Man/Zone defense. If the opposition makes a pass to the defensive rightwing area you are in a man-to-man defense. A coaching tip here would be that the defense makes their move on the first pass by the offense, after the opponents have penetrated the 28-foot hash mark. This is illustrated in Diagram 6-8. This alternating defense is very difficult to diagnose by the opponent and forces the offense to possibly change into different offenses (one for zone and one for man-to-man). It also tends to break the opponent's offensive tempo. This is a reason why I have always been an advocate of using an all-purpose offense. An all-purpose offense can be used against any defense.

When facing this type of alternating defense, the offense quite often loses its timing. Try to keep the ball out of the middle (as usual), but if it should penetrate the middle you are in the Man/Zone defense. A coaching tip would be that if the Man/Zone is stronger than your man-to-man defense have your front defensive men (X1 X2, and X3) try and overplay the offense to force them to the left.

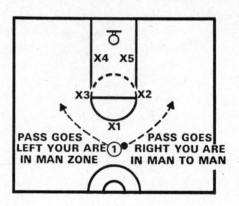

Diagram 6-8

4. You are in the Man/Zone defense. When you make a basket you change defenses to man-to-man. When you score from the free throw stripe you are in the Green 25 (1-2-2 trap at wing and posts) defense. When you miss a free throw you are in the Black 50 (1-1-3 halfcourt pressure) defense.

5. You are in a fullcourt (Green 100) pressure defense. When the offense penetrates past the timeline you fall back to the Man/Zone. Then, when the ball is passed back outside and on the perimeter (18 feet past the basket), you switch to the Blue 25 defense.

6. As long as your score remains an even number on the scoreboard you are in the Man/Zone defense. When your score is an odd number you are in the Hawk Blue 50 pressure defense. For example, if you are leading 3 to 0 you are in the Hawk Blue 50 or 1-2-1-1 halfcourt press. If you are trailing 13 to 8 you are in the Man/Zone defense.

7. You alternate defenses in regard to the position on the floor of one of your players. For example, as the offense comes down the floor and X1 lines up by the far free throw line extended, you are in a halfcourt man-to-man press situation. If X1 lines up two or three steps in front of the center circle you are in the Black 50 defense. If X1 lines up at the top of the key you are in the Man/Zone.

8. In the later stages of a game you are in the Hawk Blue 50 defense as long as you are behind. When you take the lead you are in the Man/Zone.

9. When the minutes indicated on the scoreboard clock are even numbers you are in one type of defense and when they are odd numbers you are in another type. For example if there were 6 minutes and 13 seconds remaining in the first quarter you would be in the Man/Zone. If the time remaining is 5 minutes and 46 seconds you are in the Hawk Blue 50 defense.

10. You play the Man/Zone defense following a score (field goal or free throw). When you make a turnover, play the Black 50 pressure halfcourt defense.

A VARIATION OF THE GREEN 50 (1-2-2 halfcourt) PRESSURE DEFENSE: You can use this variation of the Green 50 defense for alternating purposes in the following way. In Diagram 6-9

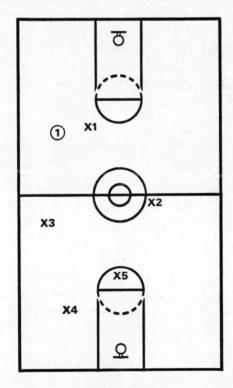

Diagram 6-9

you place your best defensive player (X1) on the offensive man who will dribble up the court. The other four defensive players line up as indicated. X1 tries to herd offensive player 1 into a trap with the help of X3. X3 is moving to a position to trap 1 just across the timeline, but he must not allow 1 to beat him down the sideline.

As shown in Diagram 6-10, X2 looks for offensive players in the midcourt area and for the possibility of intercepting a cross-court lob pass. X4 will overplay any player in his area and X5 fronts anyone near the key area. X4 and X5 would also be responsible for a long bomb pass to the lowpost area. If X1 and X3 apply good trapping procedures they will force 1 to make a high lob pass. Also, if super pressure is put on by each defensive man a 5-second held-ball call is often made.

As indicated in Diagram 6-10, if opponent 1 makes a pass to the offensive left side of the court (the shaded area), a defensive change immediately goes into effect as you drop to the Man/Zone.

Before the referee hands the ball to your shooter in a free throw situation (for example, player 1 in Diagram 6-11), have your players huddle around shooter 1 and designate one player to give the next change in defense (he can also elect to stay with the same defense). In Diagram 6-11, 1 huddles with 2, 3, 4, and 5, and after receiving their defensive change 2, 3, 4, and 5 break to their foul line positions.

THE TIP-OUT DEFENSE

This defense is quite unorthodox and it does what its name implies. Your normally best rebounders (X4 and X5) actually do not grab the rebound on a missed shot, but tip the ball out quickly to an outlet man while all defensive players break to a "tip-receiving" position. You will find that you can score baskets quickly and this will get the opponent to adjust his style of play.

Much practice time must be put in by X4 and X5 in the techniques of tipping under control. One season we had an excellent tip-out player and used this defense on spot occasions. The tip-out defense never failed to get a quick basket or two, thus frustrating the opponent.

In Diagram 6-12, when the ball is in the corner against the Man/Zone defense the rightwing (X2) covers offensive man 5 in the

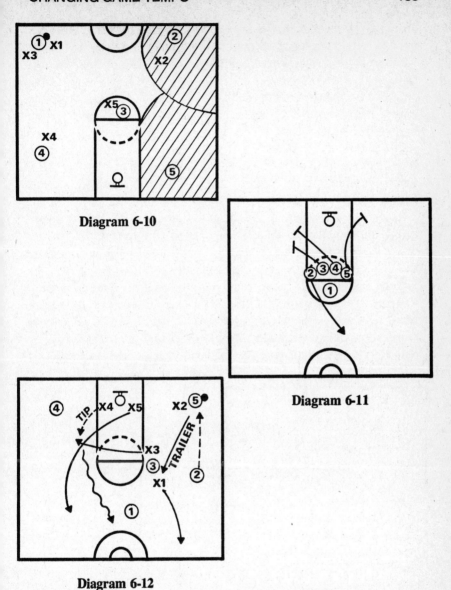

Diagram 6-10

Diagram 6-11

Diagram 6-12

right corner. As the shot goes by 5, X2 blocks him out. The weak-side rebound is tipped (not grabbed) by X4 to X3, since he has moved on the shot to an open area outside the lane. X3 immediately looks down the floor to see if X1 is open. X1 had sprinted to the opposite end as soon as he observed X4 tipping to X3. If X3 does not have a pass he dribbles hard to the middle and looks for X1 or X5 who is breaking down the left side of the floor. X2 serves as a trailer.

Again, this is a somewhat unique type of defense to alter the tempo of the game. If successful, it never seems to fail to injure the morale of the opponent.

Diagram 6-13 illustrates a variation of the Tip-out Defense formation. The Man/Zone shifts into a 2-2-1 alignment with X5 being the chief tip-out man. This is also an excellent fast-break formation. As the ball is passed from offensive player 2 to 5 in the right corner, X3 covers 5. X1 sinks to approximately the right free throw line extended. X2 sags to a near fronting position on 3. X5 moves over a step or two, being alert to front 3 if he should move to that area. X4 moves over to the weakside.

In Diagram 6-14 the rebound has gone to X5 and he "tips-out" to X1 as X1 breaks towards the ball. X1 first looks for X2 who has made his break to the far end as X5 was tipping to X1. If X1 cannot pass he immediately dribbles hard to the middle and looks for X2 or X4, who is bursting on the far left lane. X3 becomes the trailer.

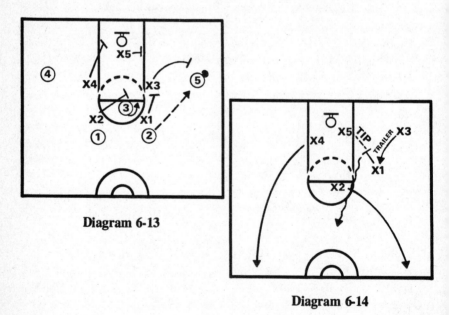

Diagram 6-13

Diagram 6-14

CHANGING TEMPO BY PRESSING OFF THE FREE THROW

The press that will be used is designated by the player who is shooting the free throw. For instance, if the Pincher is shooting you are in the Green 75 press; if one of the Chasers is shooting you are in the Blue 100 press; and if the Rover or Goalie is shooting you are in the Orange 75 press.

By using pressure from the offensive free throw you are able to place your players in an immediate pressing formation. The long bomb pass should no longer be a threat as you already have your backmen on the press in position. Each boy knows his proper formation in the pressure defense being used before hand.

One major weakness in pressing from the offensive free throw would be that you may hurt yourself in rebounding after a missed free throw. You will not always be able to put your best two rebounders in the most favorable rebounding slots. If you are a poor-shooting free throw team, you may not wish to press off the free throw. Over the years we have been fortunate to make 73% of our free throws so this has not been a concern to us. If the free throw is missed you should drop back to the Man/Zone defense.

In Diagram 6-15 the Pincher is shooting the free throw and will stay stationary as he is at the point of the Green 75 press. The Left Chaser takes the first offensive position on the left side of the free throw lane and the Right Chaser takes the first offensive position on the right side. As soon as the free throw is made the Chasers quickly drop back to their normal Green 75 positions before the free throw is taken.

In Diagram 6-16 the Left Chaser is shooting the free throw. Immediately after making his free throw he slides a few steps outside of the free throw lane at the free throw stripe extended and assumes his normal position for the Blue 100 press. The Pincher, who is lined up in the first offensive free throw space on the left side, quickly moves on the made free throw with hands held high on the player trying to make the inbounds pass. The Right Chaser, who is lined up in the first offensive space on the right-side, quickly retreats on the made free throw to a few steps outside the right free throw stripe extended. The Rover assumes his normal Blue 100 position as does the Goalie.

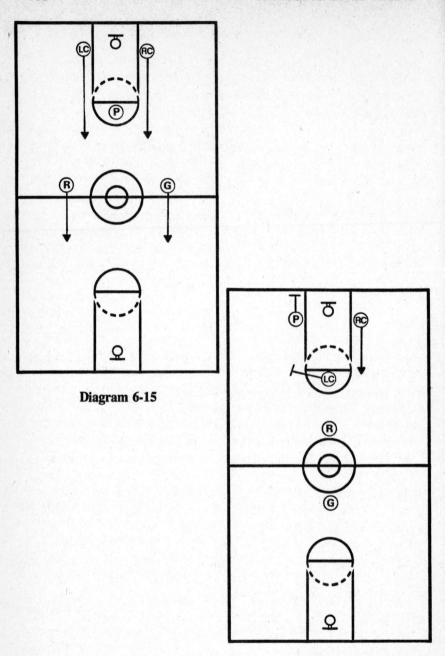

Diagram 6-15

Diagram 6-16

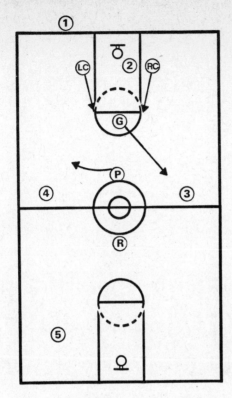

Diagram 6-17

In Diagram 6-17 the Goalie is shooting the free throw. As soon as he makes his free throw attempt he drops back to his right and takes a position near the midcourt area. The Left and Right Chasers take the front inside spaces on the free throw lane on both sides. When the free throw is being made, the two Chasers drop directly backward and occupy positions one step inside the lane at the free throw line. The Pincher moves to a position to the left midcourt area. The Rover plays deep. When either the Goalie or Rover is shooting a free throw, he may exchange duties on defense. As shown in Diagram 6-17, the offensive free throw team has adjusted to a variation of the Orange 75 or 2-1-1-1 three-quarter court pressure defense on the made free throw. The defense has actually adjusted to a 2-2-1 pressure defense since the inbounding team has two offensive players at the midcourt line.

7

IMPLEMENTING THE
MAN/ZONE FOR SPECIAL
DEFENSIVE SITUATIONS

This chapter will list and detail several "special" defensive techniques that you can use in certain strategic situations. Implementing these "specials" might win an extra game or two for you during the season and just may turn the tide for that big upset.

VERSUS THE PIVOT THREAT

In recent years the tall player has been more and more evident in basketball. All coaches recognize the value of a tall player and have spent hours and hours in developing the big man. At some time you will be playing against a team that has an excellent inside player. The rest of the team may be average however, so if you can hold down the big man's scoring your chances of a victory are good.

Your pivot defense should strive to:

1. Reduce the number of times the big man handles the ball (keep the pass out of the middle).

2. Force the big man to the least advantageous position to handle the ball.

3. Provide the strongest type of defense, individual and team, when the big man does get the ball.

4. Front the big man within 12 feet of the basket if possible (if you get caught behind a big player it is usually a sure two or three points once he receives the ball).

You can use the regular pivot coverages described in Chapters 2 and 5. But you should also have that "special" defensive alignment ready to use on spot occasions and especially when facing a super pivot threat. It just may be enough to confuse or frustrate the opponent and help you on the road to victory.

We were fortunate to win a conference championship at Shabbona, Illinois High School by upsetting a previously unbeaten opponent with the special pivot threat defense. The opponent had beaten us by 16 points in the finals of a 10-team tournament two weeks earlier. The main reason for the defeat was our inability to stop the opposition's high scoring, 6'6" post player who had blitzed our defense inside for 12 baskets.

Line up as illustrated in Diagram 7-1 and the opposition may

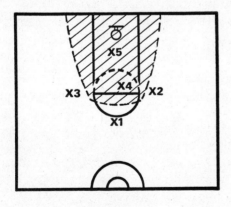

Diagram 7-1

get the impression you are in a 1-3-1 zone defense and will usually run a zone offense at you. Actually you are in a Diamond and One defense similar to the one in Chapter 5. The one major difference being that in this instance X4 (the middleman) is playing man-to-man defense on the big man. Anywhere the big man goes within a 16-foot radius of the goal X4 will guard him toughly usually in a fronting position. X5, as in many 1-3-1 zone defenses, is responsible for both corners. A coaching tip again: X4 is responsible for guarding the pivot player anywhere within the shaded area as depicted in Diagram 7-1.

When the big man goes outside the shaded area the other defensive players in the Diamond cover him as in Diagram 7-2. When he is in the shaded area, X1, X2, X3, and X5 sag and help when possible to keep the ball out of it. If the pass comes to the big man inside, he is immediately double-teamed by X4 and the defensive player in the area.

In Diagram 7-2 the big man leaves the shaded area guarded by X4 and is picked up by X5. X3 is on the weakside. X2 sags off the ball and X1 sinks to the highpost area. X4 fronts in the middle area in the lane, but is ready to pick up 4 if he should return to the shaded area. X3 is also ready to come across and pick up anyone in the right lowpost area if an offensive player cuts there. This is a vulnerable spot in this defense, as the lowpost is virtually unguarded on a pass to the corner since X4 (the middleman) is normally going where 4 is going. If the ball goes to the right corner and 4 remains in the highpost, X4 will remain there also. This weakness is shown in Diagram 7-3.

In Diagram 7-3, X4 is covering 4 (the big man) in the high post area. X5 slides out and covers 5 in the right corner. X2 sags to a few feet outside the lane area. X1 sags to the middle highpost position, but is also responsible for popping out on 1 if a long pass is thrown to the midcourt area. X3 sags to the deep weakside, aware of 3 and also alert to pick up any offensive man cutting to the right lowpost area. If 2 would cut to the lowpost on a give and go pass to 5, in this case 2 would be covered by X1 and X3 would stay on the weakside.

Diagram 7-4 illustrates a situation when offensive player 5, who is in the right corner, lobs a pass over X4's head to 4 (the pivot threat). X3 immediately comes over from the weakside and tries to

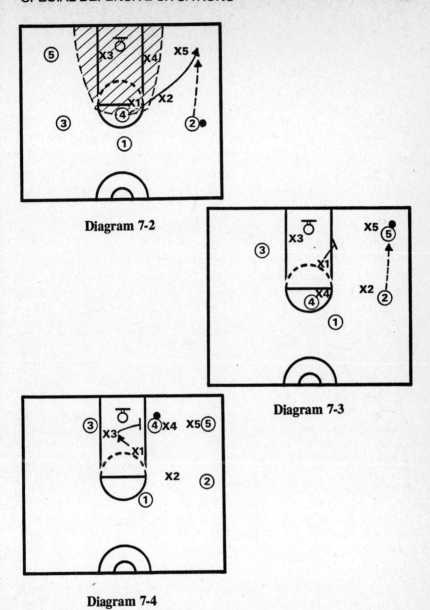

Diagram 7-2

Diagram 7-3

Diagram 7-4

draw a possible charging foul on 4 and/or double-team with X4. X1 quickly drops to the weakside replacing X3. X2 sags in the middle highpost area.

With this defense we used our 5'6" guard in the X4 position, actually guarding and fronting the opponent's 6'6" star. Our exceptional guard and the "special" Pivot Defense were the main reasons for a 50–48 upset win!

VERSUS THE STAR

Normally, the Man/Zone should be enough to stop any "star" from totally destroying your defense. Being able to slow down or stop one or more outstanding scorers is one of your tasks as a coach. In a total of nearly 400 games, the most individual player points ever scored against the Man/Zone in a single game was 44 and only three players have scored over 30 points! The 44 points were scored by a player whose team lost in an overtime game!

Whenever the high scoring star is in an area where he is a scoring threat, every effort must be made to hinder his accuracy and prevent him from improving his position for a higher percentage shot. If the star has already completed his dribble he should still be guarded very closely on his strongside, making it almost impossible for him to get off his shot. You should always have your hands up against a potential shooter. The arms should be moving in a windmill-type fashion. Players should never leave their feet unless the man or the ball is in the air. You must not stab downward in an attempt to block a shot or knock the ball loose from the opponent. This greatly lessens the chance of your committing an unnecessary personal foul.

Again, the Man/Zone should be more than adequate in derailing the outstanding scorer. However, if you wish to use variations of the Man/Zone you can use the Box and One, Diamond and One (detailed in Chapter 5), or the "Pivot Threat Defense" (described in the first section of the chapter). Another "special" defense you may wish to use is the "Stopping the Star Defense" illustrated in Diagram 7-5.

In Diagram 7-5 the defense lines up in a 1-1-2 formation with X3 playing the star offensive player (2). X1 lines up at the top of the key area, approximately 21 feet from the basket. X2 places himself directly behind and approximately 7 feet away from X1. X5 and X4 line up in approximately their original Man/Zone positions. As long as the star stays outside a 21-foot perimeter of the basket, as depicted by the dotted line in Diagram 7-5, X3 guards him man-to-man. If the star goes inside the 21-foot radius of the basket, he is immediately double-teamed by the player in the proper zone area and X3.

In Diagram 7-6, 1 passes to 2 and X3 is already on 2 man-to-man. X2 sags just outside the lane at the free throw line extended. X1 sinks to the right highpost area in a fronting position on 3. X5 takes a spot just outside the right lowpost and is ready to cover 5 if the next pass goes there. X4 moves over to the middle of the lane area and would be responsible for a lob pass to 4 in the left lowpost area.

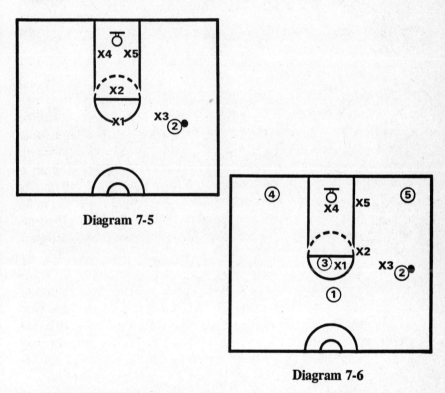

Diagram 7-5

Diagram 7-6

In Diagram 7-7, 5 receives a pass from the star offensive player (2) in the right corner. X5 slides out and covers 5. X3 stays on 2 man-to-man and is ready to defend a possible give and go cut to the basket by him. X2 sags slightly outside the lane area and X4 fronts in the right lowpost area on 3. X1 sags deep to the weakside in the left lowpost area.

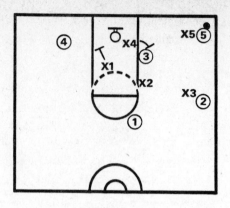

Diagram 7-7

UTILIZING THE LAST SECOND DEFENSE

This is a surprise defense reserved for use on the opposition in the last 10 to 12 seconds of a quarter. It is especially effective if you have been playing the Man/Zone and have not been using a pressure type of defense. Suddenly, you are in a pressure defense such as the Blue 100. The offense has been lulled into thinking that you are not pressing and are probably not immediately prepared to attack a pressure defense. A rule might be that in the last ten seconds of each quarter you are in the "Last Second Defense." See Diagram 7-8.

JUMPBALL DEFENSE

Organizing for possession on jumpballs is an important factor in team and coaching success. The team that has the best jumper should usually get the tap and control of the jumpball. All the formations in this section will be "special" defensive formations.

In jumpball situations the team that gains the edge may obtain the winning points in very close games. All jumpball situations fall into one of three categories: (1) potential possession to your opponent, (2) potential possession to you, and (3) potential possession is even.

Intelligence and common sense play an important role in determining who gets the jumpball. The lack of tall players is no excuse for not working hard on jumpball situations

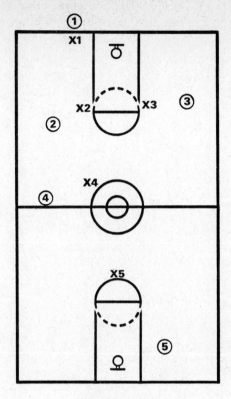

Diagram 7-8

Important points to remember in jumpball defense:

1. Most players are able to tip better and with more accuracy with their strong hand. Most players are right-handed.

2. A right-handed player will want to turn his right side to his opponent before he jumps.

3. The jumper should have his eyes focused upward on the ball.

4. In executing the jump, the off-side arm should not be brought upward. A higher jump can be executed with the tipping arm extended straight up.

5. The other jumpball players can get into the circle after the ball is touched by either jumper.

6. Before getting into position, the jumper must know where he is going to tip the ball.

7. The jumper should try and tip the ball away from the defensive man or men guarding your best receiver. If your best receiver is heavily guarded, tip to someone else.

8. Always jump and think that you can get the ball!

9. If you are jumping against a much bigger opponent you can move close to him and attempt to throw off his rhythm. You must do this without fouling.

10. You can also jump "short" and on purpose follow through with your tapping hand into the opponent's tapping hand, causing incidental contact and maybe a deflected tap. This gives your teammates a better chance at obtaining the ball. Again, you must be cautious to do this without fouling.

YOUR BASKET JUMPBALL DEFENSE: Diagram 7-9 illustrates a jumpball situation with the ball at your offensive basket. One of your smaller players (X5) is jumping. X5 should use pointers 9 and 10 in the last section. You do not want to get caught in a poor defensive setup and be vulnerable to the fast break. X4 lines up on the center of the dotted circle. X3 and X2 should move towards 4 looking for a possible interception. X2 lines up to the defensive side of any opponent in his area, in this case 5. X1 drops back quickly on defense.

OPPONENT'S BASKET JUMPBALL DEFENSE: Diagram 7-10 depicts a jumpball situation with the ball at your defensive basket. Again, one of your smaller jumpers is jumping X3. X5 and X4 must line up as indicated and prevent a direct tap to either 4 or 5. X2 and X1 line up at the free throw line extended. X2 should act like he is moving towards 5 to get the opponent's jumper (1) to tap backwards towards 2 or 3. Again, it would be a good idea for X3 to use pointers 9 and 10 in the last section. As the ball goes up X2 and X1 break at 2 and 3, attempting a possible steal.

JUMPBALL AT MIDCOURT, YOU ARE AT A HEIGHT DISADVANTAGE: The movement illustrated in Diagram 7-11 can be used by you when it is likely that 5 has the tip advantage over X5. X3 and X4 line up as shown in the offensive end of the circle. X1 and X2 line up as shown in the defensive end. Pointers 9 and 10 should be invoked by X5.

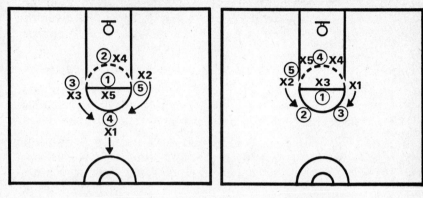

Diagram 7-9   Diagram 7-10

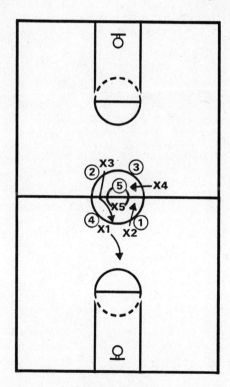

Diagram 7-11

The movement of the X players must be timed so they are not in the circle until the ball is legally tapped by the jumpers. X4 cuts in front of 3 and covers the back-tip. X3 and X2 go for the interception as illustrated in Diagram 7-11. X1 quickly drops and becomes the defensive safety.

JUMPBALL AT MIDCOURT, YOU ARE AT A HEIGHT DISADVANTAGE: Diagram 7-12 illustrates another jumpball setup when you are at a height disadvantage. X4 lines up at the offensive end of the circle. X1 and X2 are lined up at the defensive end. The main change here is that X3 is in the far left corner. Since the opponent should have to put one man back in X3's area, you have taken one of the opponent's men away from the tapping area. This is a unique formation and may temporarily confuse the opposition. As illustrated in Diagram 7-12, as X5 and 5 tap the ball X4 breaks to cut in front of 4 and X2 moves in front of 3. X1 drops to

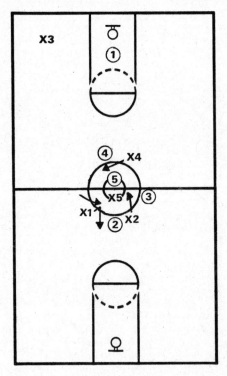

Diagram 7-12

defensive safety. Again the movement of the cutting X players must be timed so they are not in the circle until the ball is legally tapped by the jumpers.

OUT-OF-BOUNDS DEFENSE

The normal Man/Zone out-of-bounds under the basket defense is illustrated in Diagram 7-13.

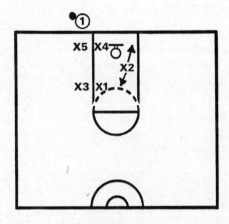

Diagram 7-13

The defensive team actually enjoys a 1- to 5-second advantage since offensive player 1 does not become a scoring threat until he comes inbounds. So, you temporarily have a 5 on 4 advantage. Underneath your defensive basket, as in Diagram 7-13, is the most dangerous out-of-bounds situation. The farther away the throw-in position from the goal, the greater are the chances that may be taken by the defensive team. Most well-coached teams have an out-of-bounds series to use when their team is given the ball in this area.

In Diagram 7-13, X4 and X5 both try to distract offensive player 1 by waving their arms, kicking with their feet, and yelling loudly in an effort to prevent an effective pass inbounds. X3 sags in slightly and protects the area to his defensive left and also, more importantly, the area directly behind X5. X1 is responsible for the highpost area but more importantly the area directly behind X4. X2 is a very key man in this defense as he must be aware of a possible sneak in behind or in front of him by one of the offensive players. X2's secondary responsibility would be to help on a lob pass to the right of the highpost area. A coaching tip here would be: do not allow the ball inside and push everything to the outside. As you can readily identify the out-of-bounds, under the basket defense is identical to the Man/Zone defensive coverage when the ball is in the corner. When the ball is passed to the outside, the defensive players easily shift back to their original Man/Zone slides.

SPECIAL UNDER THE BASKET DEFENSE: Diagram 7-14 depicts a "special" under the basket defense used on several occasions by us. If you are blessed with a tall frontline this unique formation can frustrate the opponent, especially if the inbounds passer is not a tall player. We have only had tall players in two seasons and the rest of the time our teams have averaged 6 feet and under. So you will see after reading this section why we have used this "special" defense only a few times.

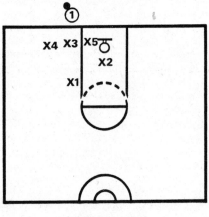

Diagram 7-14

One season we had a frontline consisting of a 6'7", a 6'6", and a 6'2" player. We placed our 6'6" man (X3), who was our best jumper with outstanding reach, directly on the ball on offensive player 1. Our 6'7" man (X5) was positioned to the right of X3 and almost in a direct line with him. Our 6'2" man (X4) was placed to the left of X3 in a direct line with him and X5. The players would jump up and down waving their arms, kicking their feet, etc., trying to distract the initial pass in by 1. X5, X4, and X3 are also very alert to an offensive player trying to split in between them or attempting to crash in behind them. X1 and X2 play in approximately the same positions as those described in Diagram 7-14, but will naturally change according to where the offense places their players. X2 is careful not to allow an offensive player to sneak in behind him on the weakside. X1 covers any lob pass in a 15-foot radius on the left side. As you can see, X1 and X2 must be fairly quick and with good anticipatory reflexes as they may have to cover a lot of territory in a hurry. You will also notice the tremendous "wall" made by X4, X3, and X5, and this may make it extremely difficult for 1 to get the ball inbounds. If adequate pressure is applied by the defensive team, frequent 5-second held balls should be called.

If the offense makes a long lob pass to the midcourt area or further, X1 and X2 should concede the pass. No damage is done in this instance and the primary objective of stopping an inside scoring threat has been achieved. To repeat the common rule: do not let the ball inside and push everything to the outside. When the ball is passed to the outside the players simply shift back to their original Man/Zone formation. The key element in this defense could be the initial surprise of the offense in seeing such an alignment.

STOPPING THE FAST BREAK

In present day basketball just about every squad uses the fast break or some form of it. The fast break will permit the team to utilize its speed to obtain the close-in shot which indicates greater scoring success.

A team beaten down the floor repeatedly by the offense will never be a winner. The zone defense, or a zone-type defense, is supposed to be weak against a fast-break team. The best weapon against such a team is to have a defensive fast break. Actually defensive preparation begins when you are on offense.

There is no excuse for a defensive team being beaten back on defense for an easy layup shot. Many coaches spend a great deal of time at practice on the offensive fast break but they seldom spend enough time on defending against it.

Specifics to work on to stop the fast break team:

1.   You should stop the fast break before it starts. If your team can hit the offensive boards, this will discourage a fast-break team. Always send at least three players, and sometimes four to the offensive boards. You should follow every shot. At worst, you may be put in a position to press the opponent's rebounder if he gets the ball. When you get the second and third shot consistently, the opposition will quickly stop their fast-break ideas.

2. You must have an offense designed to assure you of adequate defensive coverage. At every point of your offense you should have: (1) good rebound coverage, and (2) at least one safety man back on defense. Those players who are rebounders must burst back hard to the opposite end of the floor once the fast-break team has possession of the ball.

3. You may wish to pressure the rebounder of the fast-break team once he gains possession of the ball. You could put one man on him momentarily to delay him, double-team him, or actually triple-team him. Diagram 7-15 illustrates a double-team situation of a rebound. Remember, if there is no outlet pass there is no fast break. The remaining members of the team hustle back on defense

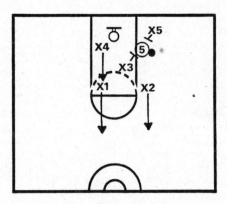

Diagram 7-15

before the ball arrives. In Diagram 7-15, opposition player 5 grabs the rebound to start a fast-break opportunity. Five is immediately double-teamed by the two closest players on the defensive team (X3 and X5). X4, X1, and X2 will hustle to the other end of the court as 5 is delayed in the double-team.

Most rebounders of a fast-break team are trained to make an

outlet pass to initiate the fast break as quickly as possible. The perfect outlet pass would be a fast on-the-line bomb. The double-team tactics will not only slow down the execution of the outlet pass, but may result in an occasional steal or deflected pass if the hands of the trappers are held high.

Again, you may wish to triple-team the rebounder or put just one player on the ball in a "one man press." The use of the latter method is usually just to delay the rebounder-passer momentarily while the defense adjusts down the court.

When a score is made (basket or free throw), many teams will quickly jump out-of-bounds and throw a midcourt or full-length baseball pass to a teammate breaking to the other end on a "sleeper" play. Frequently, if we are facing an explosive fast-break team, we will designate one player (usually a taller boy) to immediately get on the ball and overplay the inbounds passer on his strong hand while trying to destroy a long bomb pass by jumping up and down and waving his hands. In an unbeaten regular season, we recently used our center on the opponent's out-of-bounds passer. The result was that the opponent's vaunted fast break was shut off and a 58–55 victory was achieved over a high scoring team.

4. You can cut off the outlet pass. If you cannot rebound, then try to stop the first pass. If you cannot stop the first pass, then try to delay it until the rest of the defense can get down the floor. Almost all teams throw the outlet pass to the side the ball is rebounded on. The fast-break team will probably not pass down the center of the floor or cross court because this is too dangerous. So you can expect the outlet pass on the same side of the floor that the rebound came from. So, whenever possible, you should try to stop the quick outlet pass. You can do this by bursting the shallow rebounder (X2) to the ballside between the ball and the outlet man. This is illustrated in Diagram 7-16. Or, if X2 cannot get to the ball in time (which happens frequently), he must attempt to stop the outlet man from passing directly again or dribbling the ball upcourt. In Diagram 7-16, X2 cuts to a position between 4 (the rebounder) and 3 (the probable receiver). If you can intercept the pass, by all means do so. If not, see if you can tie up the dribbler-passer just after he receives the ball. Do not foul. If you cannot intercept the pass, assume the proper defensive position and keep both hands high to prevent a direct pass over your head. Try to delay the man or pass or dribble long enough to help your teammates get back on defense.

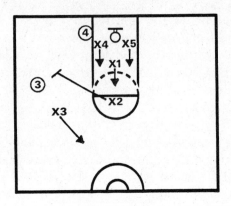

Diagram 7-16

A combination of aggressive action on the rebounder and close, tough defense on possible receivers of the outlet pass, will cause undue cautiousness in throwing the outlet pass and may destroy the fast-break team's game plan. The outlet pass initiates the action of the fast break. If you stop or delay the fast break here, you should have adequate time to get your other four defenders downcourt.

5. You can sprint the weakside rebounder hard to the opposite end of the floor. When the opponent rebounds your weakside rebounder, for example X5 in Diagram 7-16, you should immediately burst to the opposite end of the floor to help the safety man or deep defense.

A fast-break team, once they successfully complete the outlet pass, will most generally do one of two things: get the ball to the middle of the court and then fill the fast-break lanes, or move the ball quickly down the sideline. This is where a good scouting report comes into action. By using the scouting report, you can have your players move to possible interceptive positions when sprinting back on defense.

The success of the fast break may be more closely linked to a slow reaction of the defense in making the offensive-defensive transition than to the total speed of the fast-break squad.

Some pointers in teaching fast-break defense are:

1.   Have your team run their offense without any defense. Take a shot and assume the correct rebound and safety positions.

2.   Do the same thing from an offensive free throw.

3.   Run your offense against a live defense while the coach stands at the side, blows a whistle, and passes the ball to a defensive player. This is a signal for the defense to go offense and the offense to hustle back on defense. Members of the initial offensive team are not allowed to touch the ball on the coach's pass until it has been received by the defense. This is depicted in Diagram 7-17. You should have your team practice all the techniques mentioned earlier in this chapter for stopping the fast break, such as stopping the inbounds pass, pressing the rebounder, double-teaming the rebounder, stopping the outlet pass, and so on.

As shown in Diagram 7-17, the X's are on offense and they are

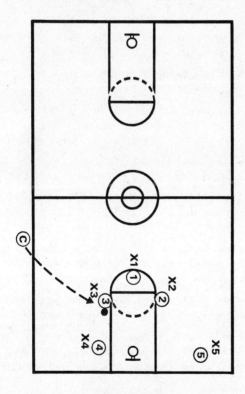

Diagram 7-17

running their regular patterns against the defense. The defense is identified by numbers 1 through 5. As the X's are going over their various offensive options, the coach suddenly blows his whistle from the sidelines and tosses the ball to defensive player 3. The X's must make the transition to defense while the numbers fast break.

4. Diagram 7-18 presents another drill that will help in teaching fast-break defense. This is called the 7 on 5 Getback Drill. The X's again run their various options, and if they score they get the ball again at midcourt. If a field goal attempt is missed or the defense (the numbers) recovers the ball by a rebound or an interception, the X's immediately retreat to defense and the initial defensive team (the numbers) fast breaks to the opposite end of the floor. The fast-break team has an added advantage because as soon as the ball changes hands, numbers 6 and 7 (see Diagram 7-18), who are on opposite sidelines from each other at midcourt, quickly sprint to the other end of the floor and join the other five numbered players in a 7 on 5 fast break. This is an excellent drill to practice for stopping the inbounds pass, pressing the rebounder, double-teaming the rebounder, stopping the outlet pass, and so on. If you can stop a 7 on 5 fast break you should not have trouble with a 5 on 5 game situation fast break.

The last line of defense against the fast break is at your defensive basket and it is much harder to stop a break here. Since the opposition has the ball in a dangerous position, you cannot take the chances that you can at the other end.

Several times during the course of a game the defense, while retreating after losing the ball, will find itself outnumbered by the fast-break team. The following are some of the outnumbered situations you may face:

1.   ONE ON ZERO SITUATION: This situation should never occur in the Man/Zone defense, but it may occasionally. You are really not in a position to do much because the offensive player is between you and the basket and, most importantly, he has the ball!

The nearest defensive player must attempt to distract the offensive player by shouting, stomping his foot, and even faking to foul the offensive player shooting the layup. The defensive player must be careful not to foul the offensive man and give him an unnecessary three-point play.

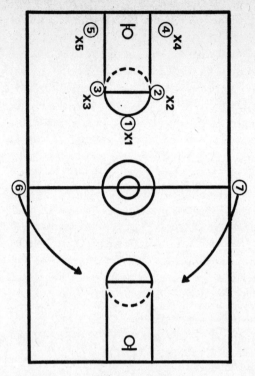

Diagram 7-18

2.   TWO ON ONE SITUATION: When a defensive player is caught between two fast-break players he must back up until he gets to the top of the key area. In Diagram 7-19, X5's main objective is to keep retreating from the key area without giving up the layup. X5 must try to slow down the two offensive players until help arrives. The dangerous man is offensive player 1, the one *without* the ball. You might have X5 fake at the man with the ball (2) to try and distract him and then quickly retreat.

If both offensive players are right-handed, try to overplay the ball to their weak hand. This is illustrated in Diagram 7-19 as X5 is overplaying 2 slightly to the left while retreating and being aware of 1.

3.   THREE ON ONE SITUATION: The defensive player must establish a position close to the goal so that he may play all three offensive men when they get in close range of the goal. The

defensive player must absolutely give up the foul line area shot. But he must try to stall in order to help and not give up the layup. Again, if possible, the man with the ball should be forced to his weak hand.

4.   THREE ON TWO SITUATION: As illustrated in Diagram 7-20, defensive players X1 and X2 line up in a tandem formation. X1 fakes at the top of the key on offensive player 1, slightly overplaying and trying to force him to pass to his left. You want the man getting the shot to be coming in to the goal from the left side if the players are right-handed. As the pass goes from 1 to 3, X2 comes out to pick him up and X1 drops to the goal area. If you can get the fast-break team to make more than two passes in this area, you have delayed the offense enough in order to get help from the other three defensive players. Again, do not allow the layup.

5.   FOUR ON TWO SITUATION: In defending the four on two situation, you should not use the tandem formation. Instead, have the two defensive players line up parallel in the lane area and attempt to delay the ball.

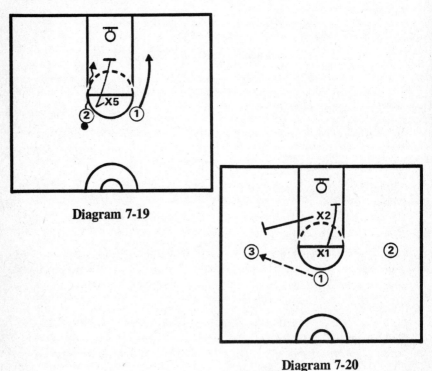

Diagram 7-19

Diagram 7-20

8

DEVELOPING
REBOUNDING FOR
THE MAN/ZONE DEFENSE

Rebounding is essential in every basketball program. The average high school team will shoot around 40% from the field and 63% from the foul line. The goal we set in our Ten Defensive Commandments (Chapter 1) is to hold the opposition under 40% from the field. In nearly 400 games, we have held the opponents to a 37.4% yearly average.

You can then figure that 6 out of every 10 field goal attempts are up for grabs to the rebounders. Four out of every 10 free throw attempts are free to the rebounders. A good rebounding team can very easily control the tempo of the game. Every rebound can be worth four points to you. If you get the rebound and score, it is two points; but if the opposition gets the rebound and scores it is two points on the other side of the ledger. Hence, every rebound can be worth four points.

REBOUNDING RESPONSIBILITIES FOR THE MAN/ZONE

When the ball is shot from a spot directly down the middle or from a position slightly to the right, as illustrated in Diagram 8-1, the rebound triangle (shaded area) must be formed by X5 from the right, X4 from the left, and X3 sliding down from the weakside wing area. X2 should move to a position in the lane, ready to pick-off a long rebound or block out anyone in this area. X1 must block out the shooter and then stay in the high key area. A coaching point here is to remind X1 that his major responsibility is to block out the shooter!

If the shot attempt comes from the rightwing, from offensive player 2 in Diagram 8-2, X2 must block him out and then stay in the key area. X1 should move to a position in the lane so he is ready to intercept a long rebound or block out anyone in his area. X5 forms the right side of the imaginary triangle and X3 forms the left side. X4 blocks out at the point of the triangle.

If the shot attempt comes from the corner, from offensive player 5 in Diagram 8-3, X5 blocks him out and then moves towards the basket looking for a possible long rebound. X2 stays in the highpost area looking for a long rebound or blocking out anyone in this area. X4 forms the right side of the triangle and X3 takes the left side. X1 drops to the point of the triangle.

Where possible, the defensive player should block out his man first before going for a rebound. When this is not possible, he should retreat to the goal for the rebound, rebounding by spot or area. The position of the ball and the formation of the offense will decide how each defensive player should rebound.

In Diagram 8-4 all players block out the offensive players in their area since they are already there. Again, if the shot goes up by 1 the triangle will be formed by X5 and X4 with X3 at the point. X2 is the shallow rebounder in the key area and X1 must block out the shooter.

In Diagram 8-5, X2 blocks out the shooter and X4 spins and closes out 3. X4 may have to pin 3 under since 3 already has an inside advantage on him. X5 immediately rolls to the basket, after blocking out 5, for a long rebound position. X3 and X1 do not have an offensive man in their area so they immediately retreat to the

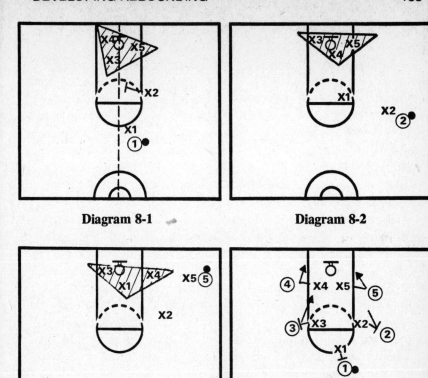

Diagram 8-1

Diagram 8-2

Diagram 8-3

Diagram 8-4

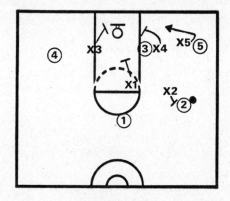

Diagram 8-5

goal. X3 has weakside responsibilities and X1 forms the point of the triangle with him and X4.

Despite being at a definite height disadvantage in a majority of our games over the years, we have been out-rebounded by the opposition in only two seasons. Other than the final score, the most important statistic in the game of basketball is a team's rebound ratio. If you out-rebound the opponent you will be a winner in a vast majority of your games. As another one of the Ten Defensive Commandments listed in Chapter 1, you should strive for a 10 to 8 rebound ratio. For example, if the opponent pulls down 24 rebounds in a game we want you to pull down 30.

In a recent championship game, we faced a team that was rated number two in the state in the preseason polls. We had defeated this team by six points earlier in the season in one of the state's biggest upsets. The final rebound count was 34 to 28 in favor of the opponent. Although out-rebounded, we had actually won the game with tremendous field goal and free throw shooting. We knew in the second game we would have to improve on the rebounding as we could hardly depend on another red-hot shooting night. In this match we out-rebounded the opposition 33–28 and despite overwhelming height disparities rolled to a 72 to 44 win!

Being a tall player does not automatically insure a good rebound position and good rebounding. However, a good big player will handle a good small player. If the big player works as hard as the small player, the big player has a definite advantage.

A 5'10" player can out-rebound a 6'4" player by perfecting his timing, position, and jumping ability. Strong defensive rebounding is one of the most important essentials of basketball defense. Against teams which show a weakness in the fundamentals of defensive rebounding, opponents may gamble with shots of poor quality because they have a good chance of getting the second and maybe the third shot.

The defensive player almost always has the initial rebounding advantage. He must maintain this advantage. If all five defensive players do their job the opponent should never receive an offensive rebound.

Since more shots are missed than made, the defensive player should assume that *every* shot will *miss* and he should be ready to rebound after each shot.

The following are helpful coaching pointers:

1. Look for a player (offensive) next to you and block him out. Get every rebound you can. Do not let anyone else get the ball.

2. There are two main methods of blocking out, both with one objective—taking away the move to the basket by the opponent. They are reverse pivot and front pivot. What may be a good block-out technique for one player may not be for another.

3. In blocking out, allow your opponent to make the first move to the basket (in most cases) and then use a quick, aggressive pivot. Use a wide base; keep elbows away from the body; keep the opponent on your back; move with short, choppy steps; forearms and hands should be held parallel to the body, with fingers spread wide and palms facing the basket ready to go after the ball. The rebounder must keep his feet moving. You should keep your arms up to (1) avoid fouling (2) protect the upper body, and (3) be ready for a "hard" rebound.

4. Once the opponent has been blocked out, go after the ball regardless of where it may be. Many players do not go after a ball they could retrieve because it is not in their area. Do not rebound by zone. Once the opponent is blocked out go after the ball wherever it is. Take a straight line to the ball.

5. If possible, have players block out as far away from the basket as practicable. This will eliminate the possibility of a taller opponent, or one with greater jumping ability, going up and taking or tipping the ball over your back. As soon as the shot is taken, the defensive players should turn and attempt to make contact with their opponents as far away from the basket as possible.

6. Your players should be aware of the following:

    A. If the shot is taken 12–15 feet from the basket the ball will normally come off the rim close to the basket.

    B. If the shot is taken 20 or more feet from the basket the ball will normally bounce out 10 to 15 feet.

    C. If the shot is taken with a high arch the ball will bounce high and long.

D. If the shot is straight and has little arch it will come off straight and hard.

E. About 75% of the time the ball will rebound to the opposite side from which it is shot.

7. Rebound the ball aggressively. Pull it in strongly and turn away from pressure before hitting the floor. Use your arms to initiate the jump. Attempt to rebound the ball at the peak of your jump, about on line with your forehead.

8. In order to insure continued possession of the ball, the rebounder must twist away strongly from his nearest opponent. Generally, try to get two hands on the ball and bring it to the chest area for protection.

9. Try to bring the ball to the chest area with one hand on top and one below to afford the best possible protection. You should land with the feet and elbows wide, backside extended slightly rearward, and weight balanced. The spread two-foot landing is essential as the rebounder will often land on one foot and lose his balance.

10. As the rebounder comes downward he should turn his head slightly towards the near sideline and look for an outlet man. The rebounder should pivot away from pressure put on by the offensive player. If the offensive player has put himself in an area between the block-out man and the nearest corner of the court, it would be much easier to pivot towards the center of the court to make the outlet pass.

11. If pressured, he should use fakes and grasp the ball with both hands firmly and pivot to prevent a tie-up and jumpball by the opponent.

12. A tall player must keep the ball above shoulder-height to keep the smaller opponent from tying him up. Do not bring the ball down low.

13. The short player getting the rebound must bring the ball close to the floor, protecting it with body and elbows.

14. Rebounding is still largely a question of courage and desire. If you combine knowledge of execution of proper technique with desire, it will produce outstanding rebounding teams and more victories.

To summarize, defensive rebounding must be aggressive and done with courage and desire. There are many techniques for blocking out on the boards. What may be a good block-out technique for one player, however, may not be a good technique for another. The defensive player should go to a spot, in our Man/Zone, and work for position. As long as your player is getting the job done do not worry about his block-out technique.

If you wish to work on a technique, the following block-out methods are preferred. In Diagram 8-6, if offensive player 3 goes to your block-out man's left the pivot will be made on the left foot. The opposite footwork would be evident if the offensive player were on the rebounder's right.

This looks fairly simple, but it actually takes some time to perfect. When first beginning, you will find your players possibly pivoting the wrong way and getting their legs crossed.

The pivot comes easy if the footwork is right. The reason we prefer the reverse pivot is that it enables the player to pick up the ball and basket immediately. The pivot must be made quickly and the rebounder must take up as much area as possible, as the objective is to block the offensive player's path. Remember the pivot must be made into the offensive man's path and *not* the man —because a foul might be called.

Diagram 8-7 depicts the front pivot block-out technique. Player 3 is trying to get to the inside and the defensive rebounder pivots on

Diagram 8-6   **Diagram 8-7**

his right foot and swings his left one around. While the reverse pivot is preferred, if your player can use the front pivot well and not lose his man he can use his own style.

A problem that may occur is illustrated in Diagram 8-8. When a defensive player, such as X5, is fronting in the lowpost area offensive player 5 will naturally have a good inside rebounding position on a shot attempt. When this happens, and any other time the offensive player gets between the defensive rebounder and the basket, you should try to have your player (X5 in this example) crowd the offensive man as close to the basket as possible. While you may not be able to get the rebound you may prevent the offensive man from rebounding also.

Diagram 8-9 shows that X3, X5, and X4 have established their rebounding triangle too close to the goal. Offensive rebounders 3, 4, and 5 are in excellent positions to grab a rebound or to tip the ball in.

Diagram 8-10 depicts an excellent block-out performance as the offensive rebounders are not in good positions. X3, X5, and X4 have blocked out the offensive men farther from the basket.

REBOUNDING THE MISSED FREE THROW

Most missed free throws will rebound close to the goal in the vicinity of the foul lane. The reason for this is that the average free throw is normally a very soft shot. Also, the rebounding triangle, mentioned previously in this chapter and illustrated in Diagram 8-11, can be much closer to the goal than the one formed for shots normally taken from the floor. It is important to be organized in order to win basketball games, and a seemingly unimportant detail such as free throw defense must not be overlooked.

As illustrated in Diagram 8-11, you should place your best rebounder (X5) in the #6 lane position on the right side. The next best rebounder (X4) should be directly across from X5 (on the left side) in the #1 lane position. X5 and X4 must line up with their feet as close to the lane divider as possible. They should keep their arms away from their bodies with their elbows outward and should follow the flight of the ball. All players should be in a bent knee position because it enables the quickest move possible. As the ball hits the goal rim, X5 and X4 must take a quick step (with the foot nearest the opponent) across the foul line and in front of the opponent. The

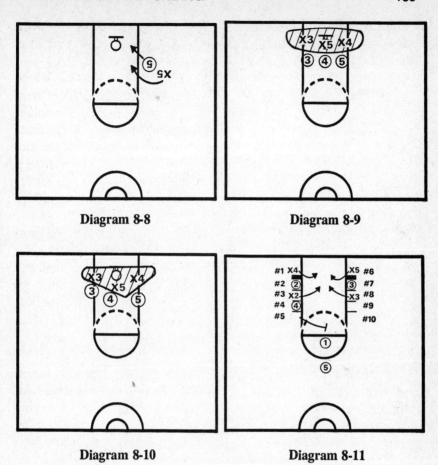

Diagram 8-8

Diagram 8-9

Diagram 8-10

Diagram 8-11

other foot follows to place X5 and X4 between the basket and the opponent. They should make slight body contact with the opponent and block him out.

Your third best rebounder (X3) should be in the #8 slot on the left side. Your fourth best rebounder (X2) should be directly opposite X3 in the #3 lane position on the right side. X3 and X2 also move in to form a cut on the boards. If the offensive team places only two players along the lane, X3 will line up with his feet nearest the lower lane divider. He should also keep his arms away from his body with elbows outward and follow the flight of the ball. Upon the ball's contact with the rim, he will quickly move into the middle of the lane to form the head of the rebounding triangle. If the offensive team places only two players along the lane, X2 will line up with his feet closest to the highest lane divider. This will give him a proper position for blocking out the free throw shooter.

If the offensive formation places a third player along the lane, X3 or X2 whichever has no opponent beside him, will take the responsibility for screening the free throw shooter (offensive player 1).

If the offensive team is putting extreme pressure on you or you are at great height disadvantage, you may wish to send X5, X4, X3, and X2 to the boards and add a fifth defensive player to the lane. This would be X1, and you should place him on the left side of the free throw lane in the #5 position. He now has the main responsibility of blocking out the free throw shooter. X1 should be your poorest rebounder. By placing your fifth man into action you automatically have a 5 on 4 defensive advantage.

Again, your primary concern should be to have possession of the ball and *not* to start a fast break. You should demand 100% possession on missed free throws.

Diagram 8-12 illustrates the correct and incorrect foot movements of a player in the #1 defensive free throw slot.

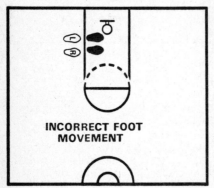
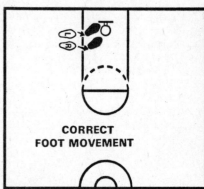

Diagram 8-12

SPECIAL FREE THROW DEFENSE

In Diagram 8-13, player X5 rebounds the successful free throw attempt by offensive player 3. If X5 is right-handed, he will normally take the ball out on the left side of the court. Players X3 and X1 are lined up in the midcourt and player X2 is in the far left corner. X2 should be a good corner shooter as he will have numerous scoring opportunities from this position.

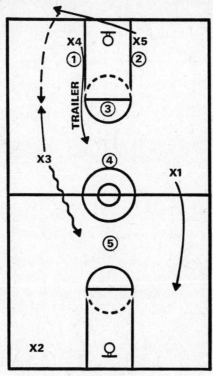

Diagram 8-13

X5 quickly steps out-of-bounds after the successful free throw and passes to X3 who breaks to meet the pass. X5 can also pass to X1 or X2 if either player is open. X3 immediately goes to the middle of the floor and joins X2 and X1 in a fast-break situation. If executed properly and quickly, there should be an automatic one player advantage and possibly a two man advantage. Another advantage may come when player 3 becomes so intent upon getting back on defense that he does not concentrate and possibly misses the free throw.

If the opponent would keep two players back as in Diagram 8-14, you may wish to use a "gap shooter" in your free throw alignment. The gap shooter is a rebounder that is stationed to the left or right of the free throw lane, behind the rebounders in the #1 or #6 positions. The rules require that a gap shooter be located three feet in back of the players stationed on the foul lane. The gap shooter must remain there until the ball has hit the rim and then he quickly attempts to enter the rebounding area. He should enter from either the baseline side or from the middle of the foul area. He should simply look for the "gap" and shoot into it.

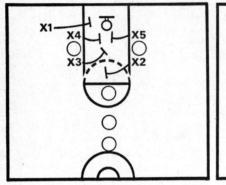
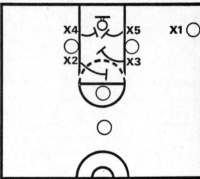

Diagram 8-14   Diagram 8-15

If the opposition were to use a gap shooter on you to attack your free throw defense, you could either line up normally on the foul lane or defend the gap shooter as in Diagram 8-15. If the gap shooter is effective against your regular free throw lineup, simply place X1 in a position to defend him. Thus, X4, X5, and X3 form the rebounding triangle and X2 blocks out the free throw shooter.

A COUNTERMANEUVER VERSUS
A DEFENSIVE FREE THROW TEAM

Diagram 8-16 depicts a situation where an opponent places only three players at the foul lane in a free throw defensive situation. This would be an effort to fast break you as the defensive team places 1 and 2 in the midcourt area.

A possible way to counter this strategy would be to have X5 spin around 4 to the outside as in Diagram 8-16. Four, upon seeing X5, may try to block out to the outside. If this happens X3 quickly shoots the open gap looking for the rebound.

As an alternate to this you might have X4 attempt to spin around 5 to the outside. If 5 would go with X4 to block him out, X3 would have the option of breaking as in Diagram 8-16 or sprinting to the left side area in 5's territory.

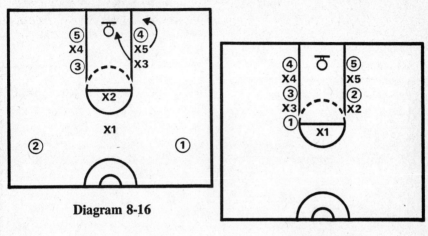

Diagram 8-16

Diagram 8-17

Diagram 8-17 depicts a free throw defensive rebounding drill that you can use for offensive purposes as well. You will find the drill very game-like and highly competitive. X1 shoots a one-on-one free throw. If he makes both, a player from the opposite team (the numbers) now shoots a one-on-one. If any player misses a free throw the ball becomes "live" and the defensive team must clear the rebound past the 28-foot hash marks. If the offensive team gets the rebound they go for the basket and a possible score. There are no boundaries and play halts when either team scores. Then the team that scored shoots a one-on-one free throw. The players on both teams rotate positions. All players must use proper free throw alignment block-out techniques. The winner is the first team to score 21 points and the losers get some sort of penalty.

Use a small rebound ring or a rebound bubble in the two drills that follow. In Diagram 8-18, X5, X4, and X3 are on inside defensive positions on 5, 4, and 3. The coaches (C1 and C2) either shoot or pass in to 5, 4, or 3 who then shoot. When the shot is taken, X5, X4, and X3 must block out to rebound. When the X's get three consecutive rebounds they go on offense and 5, 4, and 3 go to defense.

In Diagram 8-19 the defense lines up in their regular Man/Zone positions, and the offense gets in its regular positions. The coach (C) has a ball and takes a shot from one of the outside positions as indicated by the arrows. The offense works for an offensive tip or to get the rebound and the defense works to get the rebound and clear the ball past the timeline. When the defense recovers three clears, they rotate to offense with the offensive team going to defense.

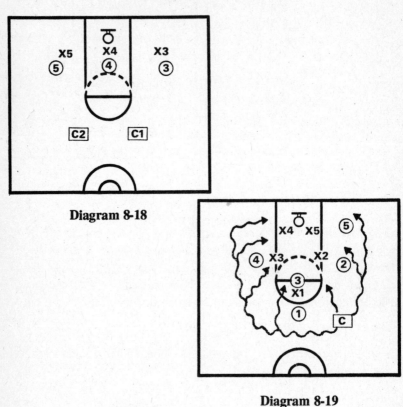

Diagram 8-18

Diagram 8-19

9

IMPROVING YOUR SKILLS
WITH SPECIAL DRILLS

Through the coach's teaching, the players must acquire a thorough knowledge of and the ability to properly execute the fundamentals of the game. The special drills in this chapter are from a list of favorites that have helped us the most over the years. The entire foundation for sound play is quick execution of the basic fundamentals of the game of basketball.

THE VALUE OF DRILLS

The following tips are for the successful teaching of fundamental drills:

1. Never use a drill just for the sake of drilling.
2. Do not give the players too much to learn. It is better to do a few things well than to have them do so much that they might not do any part of it very well.

3. For the most part, drills should be pressure simulated game-like experiences.

4. Drills should be tied in with your defensive (and offensive) philosophy.

5. The coach must motivate the players to be enthusiastic about the drill.

6. You should have variety in your drills. Run a tough drill then follow it with an easy drill.

7. The coach must explain why the drill is important.

8. Occasionally spot in a "fun" drill.

9. Make drill periods long enough for profitable learning but short enough to maintain interest.

10. Make the drills as game-like as possible, rewarding, and competitive.

You must be organized or else you cannot succeed in practices and games. Execute the drills properly and rapidly. Remember, never run a drill just to kill time. It is far better to run a few good drills properly and quickly than to run a large assortment of drills just for the sake of keeping everyone occupied.

OUR FAVORITE SPECIAL DEFENSIVE DRILLS

Point penetration drill

Diagram 9-1 illustrates a drill to get the defense to stop penetration at the point position of the Man/Zone by the offense. Allow offensive player 1 to beat X1 and X2 on the dribble and the rest of the defense reacts. If 1 splits X1 and X2, the opposite post man (X4) comes up and is responsible for stopping 1. X5 slides directly behind X4 and is ready to cover either 4 or 5 in the low post areas. X2 and X3 collapse to help on 4 and 5. X1 collapses to the ball to double-team with 4.

If 1 would penetrate to the left of X1 and split him and X3, it would be X5's responsibility to come up and stop the penetration and X4 would slide directly behind X5.

Post man exchange drill

Diagram 9-2 depicts a drill to help each post man exchange responsibilities when necessary. One passes to 4 and X5 exchanges by going across the foul line to the left low-post. X5 sees that X4 is going too high into the lane to possibly get back in time, so he calls "switch" and he and X4 exchange defensive responsibilities. When 4 receives a pass from 1, as in Diagram 9-2, X1 collapses to the ball quickly and double-teams with X4 who has come up from the opposite corner. X5 moves directly behind X4 and when he sees 5 coming across the lane the defensive switch is made with X4. X3 and X2 sink to help out if necessary in the low-post areas.

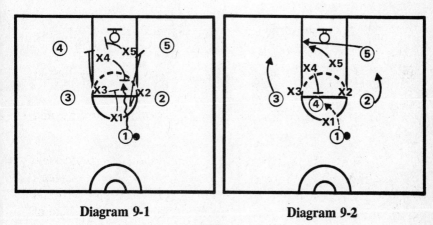

Diagram 9-1   Diagram 9-2

Pick up at lowpost drill

Diagram 9-3 is another drill aimed at alerting the weakside wing (X3) and the point player (X1) to help their teammates in a crisis. Two

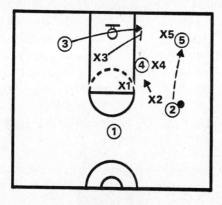

Diagram 9-3

passes the ball to 5 in the right corner and is covered as normal by X5. Four is at a medium lowpost position and must be fronted by X4. X2 and X1 are in their normal Man/Zone slides also. If 3 from the weakside would cut to the right lowpost area, X3 who is normally the weakside rebounder would have to sprint over and front him. X3 would yell "man low" and this must alert X1 to replace X3's spot on the weakside.

Midcourt trapping drill

Diagram 9-4 illustrates a trapping drill which enables the players to practice all the proper techniques of double-teaming explained in detail in Chapter 3. Offensive player 1 has the ball and he starts dribbling across the timeline as X1 and X2 quickly come over to trap him. As the trap is being clamped on him by X1 and X2, 2 breaks anywhere on the court (across the timeline) to receive a pass from 1.

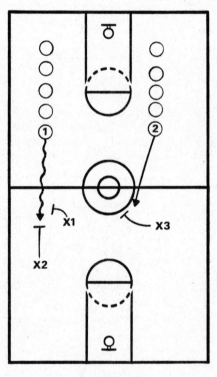

Diagram 9-4

Again, all double-teaming characteristics mentioned in Chapter 3 are used and must be carefully checked by the coach. To keep the drill competitive make a rule that the defense must get three consecutive turnovers or interceptions before a rotation is made.

Defense versus offense drill

You will find the Defense Versus Offense Drill highly competitive and enjoyed by most teams. The defensive squad plays tough defense by stopping the offense from scoring by blocking out and rebounding the missed shot or stealing the ball. When the defense accomplishes this they fast break to the other end of the floor. The offense scores in its normal ways and must get back on defense to stop the "defense's" fast break.

Points are scored in the following ways:

1 point—basket
1 point—every foul
1 point—every possession of ball (steal or rebound)

The defensive goal is to get 10 points. The offensive goal is to score 5 points. The losers run wind sprints according to how far they fall short of their goal.

Reverse pivot and rebound drill

Diagram 9-5 illustrates the proper method of applying a reverse pivot in blocking out an opponent. All the techniques described in

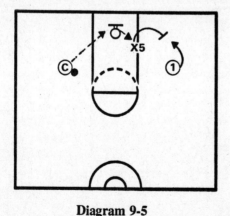

Diagram 9-5

Chapter 8 are implemented in this drill. The coach (C) has the ball and he bounces it off the backboard so it comes down on the opposite side. When the coach shoots the ball off the backboard, offensive player 1 cuts for the basket to get it and X5 must apply reverse pivot block-out techniques and then rebound the ball. Don't allow 1 to make any fakes or cut in more than one direction at first. Players exchange when X5 properly executes the reverse pivot and successfully clears three consecutive rebounds.

War drill

Diagram 9-6 depicts another highly competitive rebound drill that the coach must keep under control as play will become intense at times. Group the players into three's according to size. The coach tosses the ball off the backboard or rim and all players go to war! They proceed to tip or rebound the ball in the basket. The other two players "gang up" on the player who gets the ball. No dribbling is allowed and there are no boundaries. The three players continue to "war" until one of them gets 3 baskets. The two losers can then run a prescribed number of laps. In Diagram 9-6, X4 has rebounded and is attacked by X3 and X5.

Fronting drill

Diagram 9-7 shows a good drill to use to teach proper methods of fronting while moving from the weakside. The coach passes the ball to 1 or 3 and X5 must front 2 in the lowpost area on both sides of the lane.

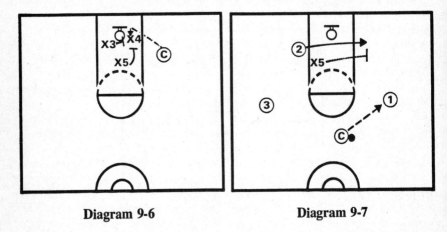

Diagram 9-6   Diagram 9-7

X5 would have to deny the pass to 2 or stop him from scoring three consecutive times to get out. Players then exchange positions.

One-on-one towel drill

Diagram 9-8 illustrates an excellent footwork drill which helps to cut down on foolish fouls. To play good defense you must be able to move your feet and not reach and grab with your hands.

The defense (X) holds a towel draped over their shoulders and takes a good defensive stance. The offensive man can use all types of dribbles (reverse, change of pace, behind the back, and so on). The

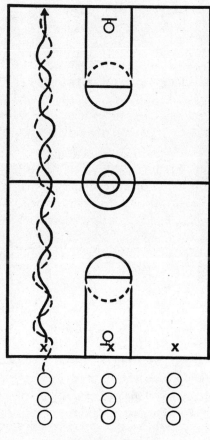

Diagram 9-8

offense dribbles down to the opposite endline and then exchanges and goes on defense on the way back.

Intercept or deflect drill

Diagram 9-9 illustrates a good drill for teaching your players the art of flicking the ball from behind and also how to retreat while in a pressure defense. On the blow of a whistle, player 1 dribbles as fast as he can with X1 chasing him from a starting position 8-10 feet behind. X1 attempts to deflect the ball from behind for a possible interception by a teammate or a possible steal.

Add another defensive player and you now have X2 and X3 chasing 2, as depicted in the right half of Diagram 9-9.

Force weakhand drill

Diagram 9-10 depicts a drill that will help your players accomplish the task of getting the offensive man to go to his weakhand side. This drill can be of value to you for defending fast-break situations or in certain defensive maneuvers in the Man/Zone defense.

The defensive man (X1) rolls the ball slowly to offensive man 1 at the top of the key area. X1 should approach 1 with good defensive techniques (stance, balance, hands up to bother the shooter, etc.). X1 must make a right-handed player go left and vice versa. He must block out after a field goal attempt and then go for the rebound. If X1 gets the rebound he goes to the end of the offensive line and 1 goes to the end of the defensive line. If 1 scores or gets his rebound he goes back to the end of the offensive line and X1 goes back to the defensive group.

Take the charge drill

Diagram 9-11 depicts a drill that teaches each player to "become a man" and take body contact from the opponent. The drill provides the player with a technique for drawing a charging foul from the offensive player. In one season our players were responsible for drawing offensive charging fouls on 87 occasions, including six in an important Super-Sectional title game that was won by us 56 to 54 in overtime.

As illustrated in Diagram 9-11, the weakside player (X1) has sprinted over, gotten into proper position, and taken a charge from offensive player 1. One dribbles three-quarter speed to the basket and X1 moves at full speed to get in the path of the dribbler.

Diagram 9-9

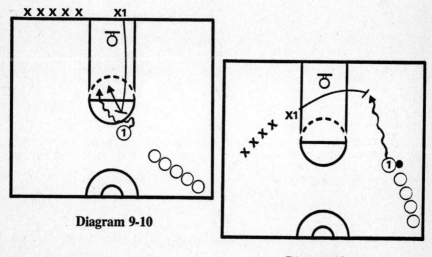

Diagram 9-10

Diagram 9-11

Take the charge off a pass drill

This is a takeoff on the Take the Charge Drill illustrated in Diagram 9-11. As depicted in Diagram 9-12, 1 dribbles towards the basket and passes to 2 as he is breaking to the goal area. X1 fakes at 1 and then takes the charge from 2 as he drives for the goal. Again, this drill is an extension of the one in 9-11 and a little more difficult to execute.

Go get 'em drill

The drill described in Diagram 9-13 will weed out your nonaggressive players. Six players (X's) line up at the endline. Place five balls at the free throw stripe. When the coach blows his whistle all players scramble to get a ball and dribble in frontcourt until the coach blows the whistle again. There is a 30-second time limit. The player who does not get a ball tries to take one away from one of the other players. The player who does not get a ball does 15 fingertip pushups or is given some other penalty. Then you repeat the game with five players and four balls, etc., until you remove all but one ball. The coach must have good control over this drill as the players will really "go get 'em."

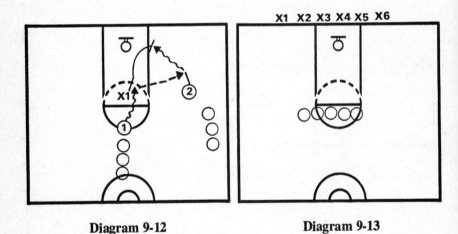

Diagram 9-12   Diagram 9-13

Defensive jumpball drill

This drill is excellent for practicing defensive situations at all baskets. Team A (your team) jumps at the midcourt circle against Team B. Put your team at an obvious height disadvantage on each tip.

You should practice all the tactics for stealing a tip as descirbed in Chapter 7. The next jumpball is at your basket and the one following at your opponent's. Keep rotating players and jumpball sites. The winner is the first team to receive 6 possessions. Because you will be at a height disadvantage on every jump, your players will really have to hustle to get the job done.

Two ball power layup with weighted ball

Diagram 9-14 illustrates an offensive-type drill that is used for getting the defensive rebounder to scoop up a ball off the floor. One stands on the free throw stripe facing the basket. On the coach's whistle, he hustles over to pick up the weighted basketball in the right lowpost area and shoots a power layup. He then hustles over and picks up the weighted ball on the left lowpost hash mark and shoots a power layup. This process continues for thirty seconds. X1 and X2 assist by rebounding the weighted balls back into their proper places. A good score for thirty seconds would be 17 made baskets.

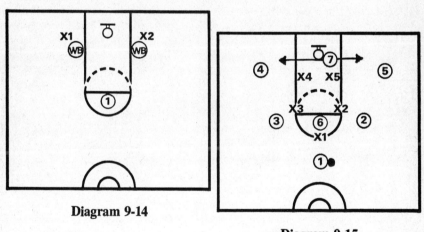

Diagram 9-14

Diagram 9-15

7 on 5 defense drill

The drill in Diagram 9-15 shows seven offensive players against the Man/Zone defense. The offense moves the ball around with the seven players approximately in the positions depicted in the diagram. Offensive player 7 runs the lowpost area looking for the ball. You will find that if you can stop seven offensive players you will probably have an easier time handling five on game nights. To stop the drill, require the defense to stop the offense six consecutive times without scoring or giving up an offensive rebound.

Hands up shuffle drill

The Hands Up Shuffle drill will help to build up strength, especially in the upper arms. Keeping your hands up on defense is a vital cog in the Man/Zone.

The entire squad lines up in groups of five, with ten feet between groups and at least six feet between individual players. This drill teaches the players to keep both arms extended above their heads and how to shuffle their feet without crossing their legs. On a signal from the coach or the team captain, the players shuffle their feet with their hands up towards the right. Then the coach or captain signals ''Left,'' ''Forward,'' ''Backward,'' and so on.

You can have the players start out by sliding and shuffling for one minute and then build the drill up to 8-10 minutes later in the season.

Run backward drill

In the Run Backward Drill the players line up in groups of five or six on the endline. On the coach's whistle, group one (with their backs towards the court) sprints the length of the floor. To make this drill competitive have the two or three groups participate in relay races against each other. This drill is a good conditioner and helps develop defensive balance.

Big man/little man shuffle slide drill

Diagram 9-16 illustrates another drill for developing good footwork. You divide your squad into groups of big players and small players. The first group (big or small) follows the path of one player as indicated in Diagram 9-16. Remember, Diagram 9-16 shows the route of just one player, but when the actual drill is run the entire group goes simultaneously. Each player shuffles his feet and slides to the near free throw line extended and back; to the timeline and back; to the far free throw line extended and back; and to the far endline and back. The first player back receives 2 points and the runner-up receives 1 point. After the first group finishes the second group goes. A player must accumulate 6 points to get out and be rewarded with a water break.

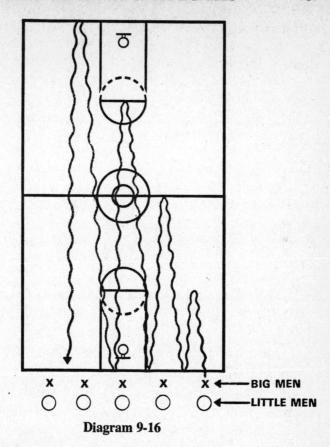

X   X   X   X   X ←——BIG MEN
○   ○   ○   ○   ○←——LITTLE MEN

Diagram 9-16

Five on two endurance drill

Diagram 9-17 depicts a defensive rebound drill with five offensive players battling your two defensive rebounders (X4 and X5). If possible, use a small rebound ring for this drill. The coach shoots the ball off the rim and X5 and X4 try to block out any man in their immediate area. All seven players attempt to rebound the ball. X5 and X4 must stay at this position until they have recovered three consecutive rebounds. The two defensive players will then rotate to offense and two of the offensive players go to defense.

Force baseline drill

Diagram 9-18 illustrates force baseline techniques detailed in Chapter 5. X5 allows offensive player 1 to go to baseline on him until he passes an imaginary line of the backboard. X4 traps with X5 on 1 by dropping quickly from his medium lowpost area. One then attempts to make a backpass to 2 or 3. X3 splits in between 2 and 3 and plays for the long pass. The defense must intercept two times consecutively in order to exchange with the offensive team. All trapping techniques described in Chapter 3 must be employed here.

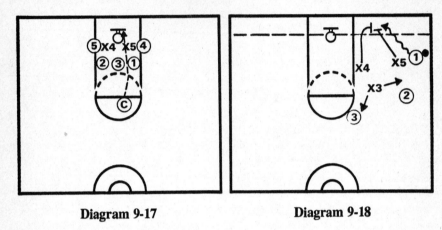

Diagram 9-17   Diagram 9-18

Two versus one and three versus two trap drills

These are excellent drills for practicing trapping techniques. Give offensive player 1 the ball and put X1 and X2 at the free throw stripe. On a whistle from the coach, 1 attempts to advance the ball against two defenders to the ten-second line. X1 and X2 execute good trapping procedures. When X1 and X2 stop 1 twice in a row, they can go to the offensive line of players and 1 goes to defense.

The same rules apply to the Three Versus Two Trap Drill.

Five offensive plays drill

The offensive team runs their offense against the defense and if they score they get the ball back. If they do not score the defense runs a fast break. Each team receives the ball for five offensive plays. You keep score in the following manner:

1. If the offense scores they get two points.
2. If the offense does not score and the defense gets a fast break and scores, the defense receives two points.
3. After five offensive plays for each team you total the score and the losers get some sort of a penalty.

10

SPECIAL TECHNIQUES
FOR IMPROVING
DEFENSIVE EFFECTIVENESS

Recently, we ran into an opponent who refused to shoot the ball and proceeded to go into a full-fledged, deep-freeze stall. We had played a tough game the preceding night and had rallied for a seven point win after trailing by fourteen points. The opponents (the deep-freezers) had not played a game that night and were well rested.

As our opponent's tactics became apparent, we decided to get the lead by using a pressure defense and then allowing the opposition to hold the ball. We managed to grab an 8 to 2 lead at the half time and they decided to "freeze" the ball the entire third quarter. With approximately one minute left in the third quarter the opposition was still stalling. For the record, with exactly 44 seconds remaining in the contest the score was 17 to 2 when they "rallied" for three quick baskets to make the final score 17 to 8!

There may be instances when you will want to counteract a

stalling opponent and still not force yourself out of your defense in a gambling manner. This would especially be true if the opposition is much quicker than you.

The "Lack of Sufficient Action" rule states:

1. When the score is tied or when the defense is behind, the defense must be continuously aggressive.

2. When there are offensive men in the midcourt area and only one defensive man goes out to pursue the ball, the defense will be warned for "lack of sufficient action." When the defense is responsible for action and the offense has two men in midcourt with the ball, the defense must have at least two men in this area. The defense is never required to have more than two players in the midcourt area. As depicted in Diagram 10-1, X1 and X2 are aggressively guarding offensive players 1 and 2 in the midcourt area. Remember, either the score is tied or your opponent is ahead in this situation; otherwise the responsibility for action lies with the offense. X3, X4, and X5 sag off their respective offensive men in the forecourt, as they are not required to play aggressively since X1 and X2 are pressuring in the midcourt area.

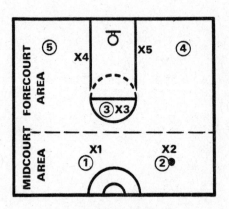

Diagram 10-1

3. A held ball occurs any time a player in his midcourt area has control of the ball for at least five seconds and is closely guarded for that five seconds.

4. After a defensive team has been warned for lack of action by an official, that team has committed a violation and a technical foul will be called for the following violations:

    A. Each time the defensive team permits the ball to remain in its midcourt area without opposition for a period of five seconds.

    B. If the team responsible for action permits the ball to remain in its midcourt area for ten seconds, during which time there is no opposing action in this area.

    C. If the defense does not continuously and aggressively attempt to gain control of the ball within ten seconds (while the ball is in the midcourt area of the opponents). If two or more players are in their midcourt area, at least two of the members of the team responsible for action must be in the area—one of whom must attempt to gain control.

The official will move to a position clearly visible to the responsible team, point in the direction that the team must advance, and call "Play ball." Only one warning shall be given to a team each period.

On a few occasions you might decide to use what we call the "Lack of Sufficient Action Defense." In a hypothetical example there may be six minutes remaining and the score is tied. Your opponent goes into a stall or a slowdown offense. Your two best players are in foul trouble, each with four fouls. Your opponent is much quicker than you are. This might be a good time for this special defense as the score is tied and you want to use up some valuable time off the clock. You also do not wish to lose one or both of your top players by a scrambling defense or a foul-prone defense.

The "Lack of Sufficient Action Defense" is illustrated in Diagram 10-2. Your offensive opponent is winning or the score is tied and you are responsible for action. X4, X5, and X3 play a triangle zone. X4 is ready to move out on 4 if a pass goes to him and X5 has the same responsibilities on 5. This defense is well within the rules since X1 and X2 are aggressively playing defense on 1 and 2 in the midcourt area. Even though 3 is in the midcourt area also, the defense is not required to have more than two players there (unless they desire otherwise) when the opponent has two or more players there. As depicted in Diagram 10-2, it may be advantageous to you to have X1 and X2 slightly overplay their offensive counterparts. This may panic offensive player 2 to throw a lob pass over to player 3, and if X3 is alert he can often intercept this pass.

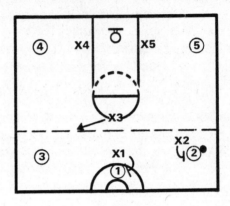

Diagram 10-2

VERSUS BALL-CONTROL OFFENSES OR THE STALL

Every team must utilize scrambling or pressure tactics to combat the stall or ball-control game employed by the offensive team leading late in the contest. The pressure defense used in this situation must be a sound one, since the defensive team must not only regain the ball but must score in order to win. A weak defense against the stall game is admitting defeat. The development of a defense which will be adequate in countering this type of game requires valuable coaching effort and practice time.

Ninety percent of the coaches who are in a zone-type formation will come out in some type of a man-to-man defense when the opponent attempts to delay action by holding the ball. We like the unorthodox and will stay with the remaining 10% of the coaches. We will stick with a zone-type pressure defense, at least until the action indicates that another option is available.

We also feel that when you are behind late in the game and the opposition goes to a ball-control offense, you can stay in a zone-type defense and still exert much pressure on the ball. You are not as vulnerable against the backdoor and layup as when you are in a man-to-man defense and behind.

An offense that many coaches feel is impossible for a zone-type team to defend is the four corner delay. We have gone against the four corner delay on a few occasions when we have trailed late in a contest. On each occasion we countered with zone-type pressure and came from behind to win. Probably the best example of going against the four corner with zone-type pressure occurred recently with our unbeaten 20–0 squad. The opponents led by fourteen points and after calling a timeout went into the four corner spread. We countered with the Blue 100, Green 75, and Black 50 defenses—alternating by signals. The result was a come-from-behind 55–48 victory!

Diagram 10-3 illustrates the Black 50 defense against the four corner. With the Left Chaser, the Pincher will guide offensive player 1 into a trap just across the timeline. If 1 is right-handed the Pincher would try to force him to dribble with his left or weak hand. In Diagram 10-3, 1 has crossed the timeline going right. As the trap is being

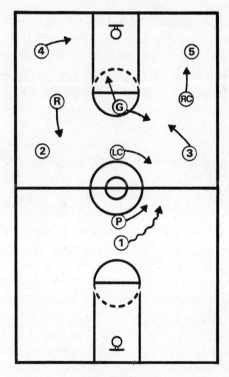

Diagram 10-3

clamped on him by the Pincher and Left Chaser, the Rover must come up quickly and be responsible for a backpass to 2. The Goalie plays in the highpost area and when he sees no offensive man there he takes on two responsibilities. He must cover 4 on a high lob pass behind him. If the Goalie has good anticipatory qualities he should be able to intercept this pass assuming the Left Chaser and Pincher have applied a good trap on passer 1. He is also aware of the possibility of 3 breaking to the middle. The Goalie should never come higher than a 21-foot radius of the endline unless he has a sure interception. The Right Chaser is responsible for the offensive player (5) in his area.

As illustrated in Diagram 10-4, a pass has been made from 1 to 3. The Left Chaser and Pincher immediately collapse to double-team him. The Goalie is responsible for 4 to his immediate right on the left side of the court. The Right Chaser overplays 5 on the right side. The Rover should play in a position between 2 and 1 for a possible interception.

As shown in Diagram 10-5, a pass has been made from offensive player 1 to 2 breaking to the middle. In this instance the Rover would move over to stop 2 and try to force him to pick up his possible dribble. The Left Chaser would collapse and double-team 2 with the Rover. The Pincher, who was originally moving with 1, will quickly drop to float in an area near offensive player 3. The Goalie will be responsible for a pass to 4. The Right Chaser is again overplaying 5 in the right corner area.

Diagram 10-6 illustrates a situation for the defense in attacking a 2-1-2 delay offense. In this type of slowdown the offense attempts to keep the floor spread and balanced and there is an interchange of positions by the outside people if so desired (1 and 5 or 2 and 4 in Diagram 10-6). You can of course keep the players stationary.

There is very little cutting in this type of offense and the object is to move the ball rapidly by using the center as a pivotal point. A good defensive alignment to counteract this offense would be the Post Trap depicted in Diagram 10-6. As illustrated, X1 overplays 1 trying to force him to the sideline. X2 fronts 3 in the highpost and X3 comes up high from his leftwing position and overplays 2. These maneuvers should force 1 to pass to 5 in the right corner.

As soon as 1 makes the pass to 5, all players immediately react to a corner trap alignment. X5 and X2 should simultaneously arrive on 5 using good trapping procedures. X1 sags and plays in between the ball

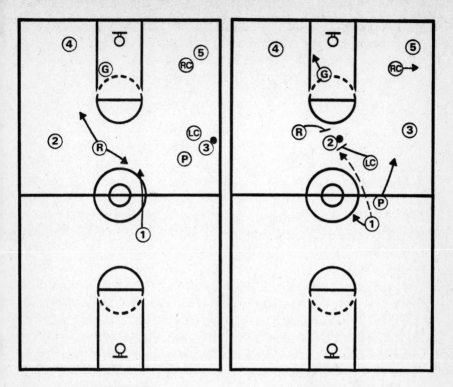

Diagram 10-4   **Diagram 10-5**

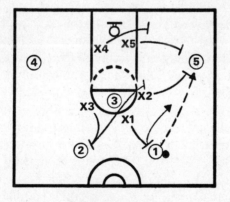

Diagram 10-6

and player 1, looking to intercept a backpass. X4 slides across the lane
and fronts anyone in the right low-post area. He must be aware of a

possible attempt by 3 to roll low or his option to roll to the weakside area behind him. X4 would be responsible for a pass over his head to the weakside. X3 quickly sags to a right highpost position and fronts anyone in that area, especially 3 if he should move there.

VERSUS THE STACK PRESS OFFENSE

Many teams are using the stack offense to confuse and defeat fullcourt pressure defense squads. You can really make use of an adequate scouting report in the defense of such an alignment. You can counter the triple stack offensive formation, as illustrated in Diagram 10-7, by using the Green 75 pressure defense. As depicted in Diagram 10-7, you would allow 1 to make the pass inbounds and the Pincher would be aware of 2 breaking high to receive the pass. The Pincher would be ready to move to the side the ball was on (in this case 2 would backpass to 1).

The Left Chaser and Rover play their Green 75 initial positions but are aware of the strong possibility of 3 breaking to the left midcourt area. They must prevent an initial long pass coming to this area from 1 or 2. The Right Chaser sags a step or two and is aware of 4 breaking to the right midcourt area. The Goalie lines up approximately 10-15 feet from 5, yet close enough to intercept a long pass attempt by 1 or 2.

If, as in Diagram 10-8, offensive player 1 is trapped by the Pincher and Left Chaser and he passes to 3 in the midcourt area, 3 would be immediately double-teamed by the Left Chaser and the Rover. The Pincher would sprint back past the line of the ball looking to pick-off a possible pass. The Right Chaser would drop towards the basket and the Goalie would stay in the goal area. The Right Chaser and Goalie must be fully aware of players 4 and 5 who will probably be in the area. If this second trap is beaten you should immediately drop to the Man/Zone defense.

If you are having trouble with an opponent's press offense and still wish to apply pressure, try the half court pressure defenses such as the Blue 50 or Black 50 or the wing and post traps off the Man/Zone alignment.

If the opponent wishes to attack with a "double" double stack alignment, you might alter your defensive formation with the Orange 75 defense as shown in Diagram 10-9. As depicted in 10-9, you would allow the pass to 1 who is breaking from the back of the stack towards the ball. Five will normally break opposite to the weakside. Three

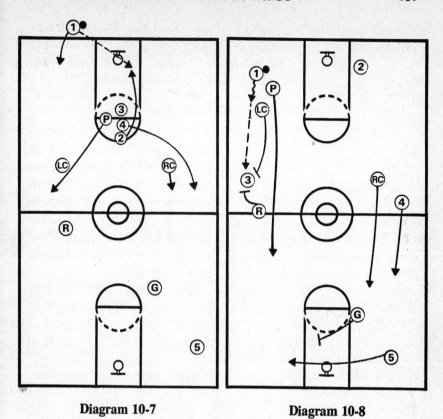

Diagram 10-7   **Diagram 10-8**

breaks from the midcourt area to the middle and 2 sprints to the right sideline.

As 1 passes to 4, as shown in Diagram 10-10, the Left Chaser and Pincher come over to double-team. The Right Chaser would float to the middle being aware of 3's possible presence there. The Goalie would sink to the goal area being aware of 2's probable deep position. The Rover would sink a couple of steps with his first responsibility being to help out deep down the floor if more than one offensive player is downcourt. His second responsibility would be to come up to help trap 4, if he should evade the trap by the Pincher and Left Chaser, or to intercept a possible errant pass. When a second trap by the defense is beaten or the ball passes the timeline, all players should drop to the Man/Zone defense.

As an alternative you may wish to attack the inbounds passer of the stack and this can be done in several ways. As illustrated in Diagram

10-11, you may wish to apply the Blue 100 and have the Left Chaser and Pincher attack the inbounds pass immediately. The Pincher initially applies trememdous pressure on the inbounds passer (4). The Right Chaser would float in the middle playing between 5 and the ball. The Rover will be responsible for covering the middle and will be aware of 3's possible presence in this area. The Goalie can cheat up a few steps and can break up to intercept a pass to 2 if he is absolutely sure he can get the ball!

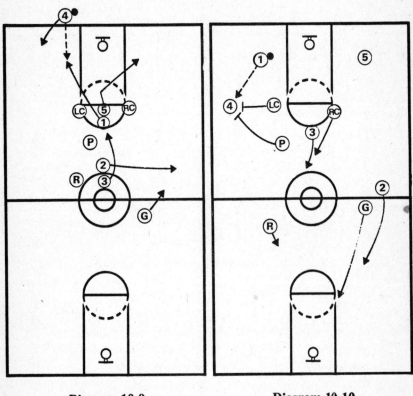

Diagram 10-9   Diagram 10-10

Another defensive option, illustrated in Diagram 10-12, would be to have the Pincher apply the usual pressure on 4. The Left Chaser would play with his back to the ball and cover the first offensive player breaking to his side of the floor (in this case 1) and overplay him. The

Goalie would come up, being careful not to be backdoored and cover player 2.

If extreme pressure is applied, the offensive team may be forced into a five-second inbounds violation and thus lose possession of the ball. In this defense it would be best if once the ball is inbounded, the two nearest defensive players would trap it and the remaining players would fall into Blue 100 pressure defense positions.

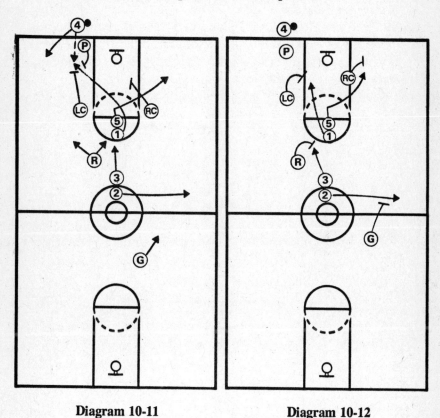

Diagram 10-11   **Diagram 10-12**

ZONE PLUS ONE SURPRISE PRESS

This is a "surprise" press that is actually a four player zone and one player (the Goalie) playing underneath the basket. This is a good press if your team is one that has four relatively good press players and one player that is a poor presser, probably your big, slow man. You

would station him under the basket to stop all fast-break layup attempts
and he would of course be in an excellent rebounding position.

As illustrated in Diagram 10-13, the Pincher lines up near the free
throw line extended and stays to the side of offensive player 2 as he
dribbles downcourt. When 2 crosses the timeline he is immediately
double-teamed by the Pincher and the Left Chaser. The Pincher and
Left Chaser must arrive simultaneously, while applying all the trapping rules to try and force a lob pass by 2. The Rover and the Right
Chaser look for possible interceptions, especially being aware of the
positions of players 4 and 5. The Goalie remains at "home" and is
ready to stop all fast-break situations. If the trap is broken the players
fall back to the Man/Zone defense.

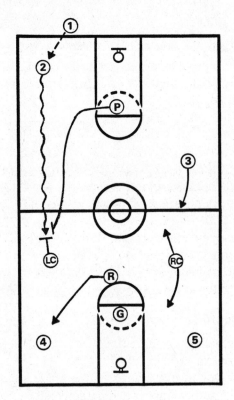

Diagram 10-13

TREASURE CHEST OF 21 MAN/ZONE SECRETS

The following have been successfully used at some time or another by the author. Ninety percent of these methods are still being used today.

1.   Mini-scorecard

This is a chart to be kept by your assistant coach and is shown in Diagram 10-14. Many times in our early years of coaching, assistant coaches and I found ourselves asking such questions as: Are we in the bonus situation yet? How many fouls on their center? Is that their last timeout? Instead of having to run down to the scorer's bench to get this sometimes game-saving information, you can have it right at your fingertips. The answer is the mini-scorecard.

Your assistant coach should constantly double-check with the official scorer during the course of the game. During the first two or three minutes of the half time break he can summarize the chart giving you a quick review.

Information kept on the front of each card includes: team fouls for each team for each half; timeouts for each team; names of players for each team; numbers of the players; individual player fouls; baskets and free throws. On the back of each card you may keep such information as: the opponent's defensive and offensive alignments for each quarter of the game; your team's offensive and defensive alignments for each quarter; notations on the quality of the officials for future reference.

You will find your evaluations and notations especially valuable if you are playing this team later in the season and wish to look back to see what worked or did not work in your first meeting. You will also find it useful to refer to the alignments from one year to the next.

2.   Pizza for under 50 points per game

We have a standing rule that any time we hold an opponent under 50 points in a game the coaching staff foots the bill for a pizza party. The players show great interest along these lines and have nearly driven the coaching staff to bankruptcy. For example, one of our squads which was ranked number one in the state held 17 opponents under 50!

Mini-Scorecard
Front of Card

Name	Opponents No.	Fouls	Scoring	Name	Anderson Highland No.	Fouls	Scoring

First Half	*Timeouts*	*Second Half*
Team Fouls		Team Fouls
We 1 2 3 4 5	We 1 2 3 4 5	We 1 2 3 4 5
They 1 2 3 4 5	They 1 2 3 4 5	They 1 2 3 4 5

Our Offense   Opponent's Offense

Our Defense   Opponent's Defense

Officials _____

| Excellent | Good | Fair | Poor | Excellent | Good | Fair | Poor |

Back of Card

Diagram 10-14

3. Mr. Hustle and Mr. Defense boards

We got this idea while attending a clinic a few years ago. A board, which can easily be made in your industrial arts department, is placed on the wall in the gym and lists the season schedule and the winners of the Mr. Hustle and Mr. Defense awards for each game. The winner of the Mr. Hustle award is determined by the total number of assists plus the total number of steals in a particular game. You then subtract the number of individual turnovers for each player. For example, if your center had two assists, five steals, and committed two turnovers he had a final total of five. The Mr. Defense award winner is decided by the total number of rebounds for the individual player minus his turnovers. At the bottom of the board you may list your accumulated season leaders in steals, rebounds, and assists. (See Diagram 10-15.)

4. Defensive pennants or banners

A defensive pennant is displayed in the gym for any special defensive honor bestowed on your team, such as Number One Defensive Team in the State 46.1, and so on. You can use different color pennants to denote different defensive titles. For instance, for a conference defensive championship the pennant is blue; for the area defensive championship red; and for the state defensive championship white. (See Diagram 10-16.)

5. Player of the week defensive award

The defensive player of the week, selected by the team or coaching staff, is honored by having his picture displayed for a week in a trophy case which is in full view of the student body. Another alternative for selecting the "Defensive Player of the Week" is by using statistical charts, such as the Player Evaluation Chart detailed in Chapter 1 or the Simplified Defensive Chart mentioned later in this chapter.

6. Different color wristbands

The top rebounder and the top defensive player in a game would wear different color wristbands in the next game. For example if the team wears red wristbands, the top rebounder would wear a set of blue wristbands in the next scheduled contest and the top defensive player would wear a set of white wristbands in the next game.

MR. HUSTLE		MR. DEFENSE
PLAYER	OPPONENT	PLAYER
	(DALEVILLE)	
	(FRANKTON)	
	(MADISON HTS)	
	(YORKTOWN)	
	(WES DEL)	
	(ANDERSON)	
	(MISSISSINEWA)	
	(WESTFIELD)	
	(LAPEL)	
	(DELTA)	
	(FRANKTON)	
	(PENDLETON HTS)	
	(ALEXANDRIA)	
	(MADISON GRANT)	
	(MUNCIE CENTRAL)	
	(PENDLETON HTS)	
	(SHENANDOAH)	
	(JAY COUNTY)	
	(MOUNT VERNON)	
	(ELWOOD)	

1st Steals	
1st Rebounds	
1st Assists	

Diagram 10-15

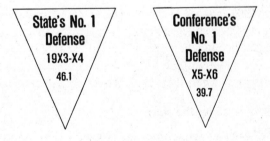

State's No. 1
Defense
19X3-X4
46.1

Conference's
No. 1
Defense
X5-X6
39.7

Diagram 10-16

7. The use of half time statistics

At half time the coach should "call out" the number of defensive (and offensive) rebounds for each player. This lets the entire team know who is getting the job done and who isn't. For example, if your number one rebounder who averages 15 rebounds per game has only two rebounds at halftime—he should know about it! Any defensive lapses or weaknesses that must be corrected are also pointed out.

8. Embroidered jock

The player who makes the most interceptions or steals in each game is presented with the embroidered jock award. The home economics department cooperates with us in this venture by embroidering the jock. You will find that the players actually look forward to receiving this "honor."

9. Rain boots

In our early years of coaching we had the players wear rain boots at practice. On "Rain Boot Night" the players put the boots on right over their gym shoes. This is an excellent conditioner for the legs. We have also had the players use ankle weights which can easily be strapped to the ankles. Other exercises used to build leg muscles are running the bleacher stairs and bench jumps. For bench jumps you should use a normal dressing room bench or a board stabilized between two chairs. The player stands at the side of the bench and then jumps sidewards and over it. As soon as his feet touch the floor on the other side he immediately jumps back over again. The outstanding jumper can do about 35 bench jumps in a 30-second time limit.

10. Shiny gloves or painted gloves

In our early years of coaching we would sometimes bring five pairs of shiny-colored work gloves for the "defensive team." This is a device to get the players to see the value of keeping their hands up on defense. When playing the Man/Zone they can readily tell when the arms are up and when they are down.

11. Putting stars on the warm-ups

The offensive high scorer usually gets the glory. I had noticed that a high school football team was rewarding its players by placing stars on the helmets of those who had recovered fumbles, intercepted passes, and so on. These stars were great for motivation since everyone watching the game could tell which player was making the outstanding defensive plays. So, with the cooperation of the art department we decided to award felt stars for the big defensive basketball plays. The stars can easily be sewn on the inner or outer warm-up of the uniform and are awarded each game for the following:

A player who makes three steals gets 1 star

A player who takes two defensive charges gets 1 star

A player who gets 10 defensive rebounds gets 1 star

A player who gets 6 offensive rebounds gets 1 star

A player can lose a star by committing 3 errors or turnovers, by being beaten on the baseline, for not getting hands up on defense, and so on.

We award the stars in a special ceremony on the first and third Monday of every month. If one or more varsity players, managers, statisticians, or cheerleaders has a birthday during the month we also have a party honoring the birthday individual or individuals. We invite the cheerleaders to the last portion of practice and soft drinks and cake are served. This is an excellent time for presenting the defensive stars to the players.

While birthday parties may sound a bit corny to you, we have found that such get-togethers are excellent for morale and tend to bring the team closer together. For instance, you will probably find the players reminding you of their or their teammates' birthday dates.

12. Simplified defensive chart

This is a chart compiled after the game, and kept by an assistant coach or a competent statistician, which evaluates an individual player's performance during a game. This chart is the same as the Individual Player evaluation Chart detailed in Chapter 1. As illustrated in Diagram 10-17, points are given for a basket (2 points), free throw (1 point), assist (1 point), and so on. Points are taken away for a foul (−1 or −2 points), an error or turnover (−3 points), and so on.

If you are in a man-to-man defense you simply subtract the number of points that were scored by your player's opponent. For example, if your center's opposing pivot man makes 23 points your center receives a −23 in this category. If you are in the Man/Zone, you can either divide the total points scored by the opposition against you or you can chart what area the opposition is scoring in and place the responsibility by area.

At the bottom of the card is a spot for rating your players (excellent, average, poor) in the categories of aggressiveness, hustle, and teamwork.

```
PLAYER _____    GAME _____
    BASKET +2 .............................. _____
    FREE THROW +1........................... _____
    ASSIST +2 .............................. _____
    REBOUND +2 ............................. _____
    STEAL +1 ............................... _____
    TOOK A CHARGE +2 ....................... _____
    FORCED A HELD BALL +1 .................. _____

    FIRST TWO FOULS −1 ..................... _____
    LAST THREE FOULS −2.................... _____
    TURNOVER −3 ........................... _____
    OPPONENTS PTS. −1 ..................... _____
    BEATEN ON BASELINE −1 ................. _____
    DID NOT FIGHT THRU SCREEN −1.......... _____

    TOTAL _____

                        EXCELLENT   AVERAGE   POOR
    AGGRESSIVENESS
    HUSTLE
    TEAMWORK
```

Diagram 10-17

13. Play by play defensive chart

One season we listed our assistant coaches as offensive coach and defensive coach. Too often the assistant basketball coach's duties are unclear. He is sometimes a cheerleader, scorekeeper, trainer, and sometimes has no more value than a bump on a log. So, try to get your assistant coaches into the action. We help to accomplish this by making the assistants responsible for keeping the Play by Play Defensive Chart illustrated in Diagram 10-18. The coach can inform the players of their

Attendance 9600

PLAY BY PLAY DEFENSIVE CHART   (23-0)   (17-6)

Date ___3/13/76___ Anderson Highland vs. Carmel at Anderson Regional

FIRST QUARTER

7:13 Lantz was beaten on baseline.

6:47 Egger does not have hands up

3:08 Sanders outhustled on boards

Turnovers

:04 Lantz traveling

SECOND QUARTER

6:10 A. Richie offensive rebound taken over your back

2:57 Sanders did not block out shooter on free throw

7:10 Poole 3 seconds
          lane vio.

5:46 Lantz bad pass

1:05 A. Richie bad pass

:41 Poole stepped
          out of bounds

THIRD QUARTER

5:13 Sanders did not follow shot

:26 Poole did not front in low post

FOURTH QUARTER

6:19 Poole hands not up on defense

3:54 Egger beaten on weakside rebound

3:20 Egger bad pass

                  OVERTIME

1:58 A. Richie foolish foul for reaching

Total Turnovers ___6___

Total Defensive
      Miscues ___10___

SCORE BY QUARTERS:

CARMEL   OVERTIME
                    8 7 17 13 6 = 51

ANDERSON HIGHLAND   7 6 16 16 14 = 59

SCORING SUMMARY:

ANDERSON HIGHLAND (59)

	SA-B	FTA-FT	Pts.
Egger	4-3	0-0	6
A. Richie	12-6	8-4	16
Poole	11-4	10-10	18
Sanders	6-1	1-0	2
Cook	0-0	0-0	0
Lantz	15-5	7-7	17
	48-19	26-21	59

CARMEL (51)

	SA-B	FTA-FT	Pts.
Herrmann	13-5	10-9	19
Kein	3-1	0-0	2
Hensel	9-7	3-0	14
Burrell	7-3	0-0	6
Leonard	16-3	0-0	6
Ogle	1-1	2-2	4
	49-20	15-11	51

Key:

SA - Shots Attempted   B - Shots Made   FTA - Free Throws Attempted

FT - Free Throws Made

Pts. - Points

Play by Play Defensive Chart

Diagram 10-18

defensive errors at timeouts and at half time. As you can see, the exact time of the turnover or defensive mistake is listed according to player.

14. Little things defensive chart

This is still another chart for one of your assistants to keep during the course of a game. The Little Things Defensive Chart is depicted in Diagram 10-19. It concentrates on "little things," but these are very important details that are not kept by many teams. As shown in Diagram 10-19, the top fourth of the chart depicts the offensive and defensive miscues made by a player or team. The second fourth is a report on all possessions (by both teams) that result in no shots, one shot, two shots, or three or more shots. The third fourth is a summary of the first fourth, listing individual player defensive and offensive miscues by categories and the last fourth of the chart illustrates free throw, jumpball, and out-of-bounds performance tallies.

15. Defensive checklist

It is wise for each coach to have a defensive (and offensive) checklist for reviewing what is necessary before the first game and during the season. It's too easy to overlook some important phase of the coaching program, and thus a checklist which can be reviewed from time to time is most essential. A defensive Checklist is illustrated in Diagram 10-20.

16. Evaluation of teammates chart

We have used the Evaluation of Teammates Chart, or a similar version, in each of my years as a head coach. It has proven quite helpful in detecting problems among players. Such cancers to team development as personality clashes or conflicts may be brewing.

You should only allow five to eight minutes for answering the questions since speed seems to provide a more accurate measurement. The evaluation should be issued to the squad without prior warning. After they have been filled out, collect the unsigned charts and transfer the results to a master sheet. You and your assistant coach should also fill out evaluations.

As illustrated in Diagram 10-21, there is also a spot on the chart for the players to rate their teammates according to all-around ability. The players should *not* rate themselves. At the bottom of the chart is a place for the player to vote for his top two choices for team captain.

Little Things Defensive Chart

Date _____   vs. _____   Quarter _____

Offensive and Defensive Miscues

D E F E N S E	
O F F E N S E	

No Shots	One Shot	Two Shots	3 or More		No Shots	One Shot	Two Shots	3 or More	

Player No.	Turnovers	Not Hands Up	Not Hustling	Not Following Shot	Beaten on Baseline	Not Fronting	Poor Rebounding		

Free Throws		Jumpballs		Out-of-Bounds			Under
Missed 1 + 1	Missed 2nd Shot 1 + 1	Our Possession	Opponent's Possession	We Tried	We Scored	They Tried	They Scored

Diagram 10-19

DEFENSIVE CHECKLIST

_____ Employ the Man/Zone effectively

_____ Employ various zones effectively

_____ Employ various combination defenses effectively

_____ Employ fullcourt and three-quarter court pressure
_____ effectively

Employ halfcourt and quartercourt pressure effec-
_____ tively

_____ Able to implement special pivot coverages

_____ Employ the force baseline defense effectively

Employ changing and alternating defenses effec-
_____ tively

_____ Employ special defenses to stop the ''star''

_____ Able to utilize the ''last second defense'' effectively

_____ Employ jumpball defense at all three circles

Employ out-of-bounds defense (under and side) ef-
_____ fectively

_____ Employ defense to stop the fast break

_____ Employ defense to stop ball-control or stalling teams

_____ Employ regular and special free throw defense

Diagram 10-20

EVALUATION OF TEAMMATES CHART

Do *not* include yourself in this evaluation.

1. List the 3 players who always take good shots.
2. List the 3 best shooters
3. List the 3 best rebounders
4. List the 3 best drivers

Diagram 10-21

5. List the 3 best passers
6. List the 3 best defensive players
7. List the 3 best offensive players
8. List the 3 best hustlers
9. List the 3 quickest players
10. List the 4 players you most like to play with
11. Who is the friendliest on-and off-court player?
12. Who is the calmst and coolest in a tight game?
13. Who is the best team man?
14. Who believes most in team success?
15. Who is the hardest player to guard?
16. List the 3 players who habitually take bad shots
17. List the 3 poorest shooters
18. List the 3 poorest rebounders
19. List the 3 poorest drivers
20. List the 3 poorest passers
21. List the 3 poorest defensive players
22. List the 3 poorest offensive players
23. List the 3 poorest hustlers
24. List the 3 players who are the slowest
25. List the 4 players you least like to play with

Rate the players 1 to 11 (1 is best) *according to all-around ability*. (Do *not* include yourself in this rating.)

Bruce Cook	Ronnie Knotts
Ed Cupp	Rick Lantz
Tom Egger	Dave Poole
Randy Hollon	Adrian Richie
Jeff Jamerson	Terry Richie
Mickey Kessler	Brian Sanders

*My first choice for team captain is*_____(2 points)
*My second choice for team captain is*_____(1 point)

Diagram 10-21 (continued)

17. News media and scrapbook

Spectators usually voice greater approval for offensive play than for defensive play. The wise coach will make a series of mental notes during the course of a game on the outstanding defensive plays of his men. He should then pass these "bouquets" out to the news media after the game. We like to give mention to these defensive "stars" at every opportunity.

You can also have a manager keep a season-long scrapbook with the defensive gems underlined in red. My wife has always kept the scrapbook for our teams.

18. Feeder program

Many coaches fail to realize it, but the heart of a successful basketball program is in the lower-level feeder schools. Practice does not make perfect—especially if you practice the wrong fundamentals.

All teams lower than the varsity level play only the man-to-man defense. During the summer, we run an annual two-week camp for students entering the 7th, 8th, and 9th grades in the fall. At the camp the emphasis is on defense—especially on defensive stance, man-to-man basics, and rebound position. Most of the work is done by rotating the players to various stations. Guest coaches are brought in and basketball instructional films are used. We annually award Mr. Defense and Mr. Hustle trophies and a few offensive awards. In addition, each boy is presented with a "Future Champions" T-shirt.

This clinic, which is strictly nonprofit with all coaches donating their time, has been successful for several years. On the final night we invite the parents to an awards ceremony where the trophies are presented and each player participates in a 10-minute all-star game. Each grade level also participates in a 10- to 12-game summer league schedule with neighboring schools in conjunction with the clinic.

We have our elementary school teams come in at different times in the season and play at half time at one of our home varsity games. We also invite the boys into the locker room before the game.

19. End-of-season defensive awards

At our annual team banquet given by the Parents Club at the end of the season, we award the following trophies for defensive prowess: Mr. Hustle, Top Rebounder, and Most Steals.

20. Basketball manual

For a basketball program to be effective, the thinkings and teachings of each coach in the system must closely parallel those of the head coach. This is easy to state but very difficult to achieve. The primary purpose of the Manual is to standardize the teaching of as many phases of basketball as possible.

The Manual should include what is to be taught, how it is to be taught, and the drills for mastering the skills.

An outline of our Basketball Manual follows:

1. Table of Contents
2. Calendar (October to March)
3. Offensive Checklist
4. Defensive Checklist
5. Offensive Syllabus
6. Defensive Syllabus
7. Drills (Passing, Dribbling, Conditioning, Shooting, Rebounding, etc.)
8. Special Defenses
9. Press Offenses
10. Pressure Defenses
11. Out-of-Bounds Plays
12. Jumpball Plays
13. Players' names, Addresses, and Phone Numbers
14. Special Phone Numbers (Press, Radio, VIP's, etc.)
15. Underclass Schedules
16. National Free Throw Contest Results
17. Officials' Ratings and Phone Numbers
18. School Records (Individual and Team)
19. Morning Free Throw Chart
20. Equipment Inventory (Issued and In-Stock)

In conjunction with the Basketball Manual, we have had successful results with a Player Handbook, Pre-season Player Conferences, and Preseason Parent Visitations.

PLAYER HANDBOOK: Includes the following: Practice Procedures, Locker Room Tips, Training Tips, Rules, Anderson Highland Offense, Anderson Highland Defense, Traveling Tips, Classroom Conduct, Public Relations Policy, Anderson Highland Honor Roll (players playing college basketball, team and individual records, season schedule).

PRESEASON PLAYER CONFERENCES: Emphasis on our philosophy of basketball, the player's goals, his ambitions, his weaknesses, his ability, his relationship to teammates, his possible selection of a college, and outside problems. The main theme should always be that you must have team spirit—team before individual spirit.

You should get to know the players as well as you can. After they graduate try to follow-up on them and their careers.

PRESEASON PARENT VISITATIONS: Give the parents a copy of the Player Handbook and review the same things you have gone over with the players. This way the parents get to know you a little better and also get to know your rules. Parents cannot say that they were not aware of the rules, since placing them down in a handbook leaves no doubt in anyone's mind.

21. Defensive scouting

If you are close to your opponents in ability, a sound scouting report and proper use of information can make the difference between victory and defeat. I firmly believe that a scouting report is a must at any level of play. It can help you upset a superior opponent, it will build morale, and most importantly it will help you win games.

Get all the pertinent facts down on paper. Avoid guesswork whenever possible. Try to scout a team more than once as a single look seldom suffices. If possible, look up the opponent team's statistics and analyze them.

You should use the following for defensive basketball scouting:

1. If at all possible, scout the game yourself. You know your team's strengths and weaknesses better than anyone else.

2. If possible, get to the game early. Try to sit as high up in the bleachers as you can to get a clear view of the court.

3. During warm-up time, write the numbers of the players down and watch them shoot. Note their favorite spots for shooting.

4. Chart the little things, such as out-of-bounds plays (both side and under), jumpball formations, and anything special.

5. Diagram the offensive setups of the opponent.

6. At every timeout, use the time to assess the opponent.

7. At half time, check your report to see if you have left anything out. If possible, discuss the game with others.

8. During the second half, look for adjustments or anything new in the offensive alignment.

9. After the game is over, write up your report immediately while scouting points are still fresh in your mind.

Diagram 10-22 illustrates a partial form for one of our defensive scouting reports.

As coach, you should make every effort to encourage team play. You don't have to worry about motivating the player who scores 25 points a game. It's the player who contributes just as much in the way of defense and rebounding who ordinarily needs recognition. You can reward these players by playing them up in the news media and through award systems mentioned earlier in this chapter. It's great to have a high scorer on your team. It's even greater to have five or more kids who play together and sacrifice for one another for the betterment of the team. A team such as this can compensate for all sorts of physical shortcomings.

A coach must use every method at his disposal to build both individual and team pride. Since pride is an intangible asset, it cannot be physically displayed to your players. If you have to provide an example, just have them look at the constant winners. All of them have pride to spare!

Coaches and teams build reputations with high-powered offensive systems, but they *win* games with a good *defense*.

DEFENSIVE SCOUTING REPORT

Team Scouted _Madison Heights_ vs. _Richmond_ at _Anderson_

Score by Quarters:
R 18 15 13 17 = 63
MH 13 20 13 21 = 67

Our Matchup
Lantz 6-4 200
Richie 6-0 155
Poole 6-2 153
Egger 6-2 146
Sanders 5-10 142

STARTING LINEUP
#44 Falker 6-5 205
#32 Terry 6-4 200
#43 Tolbart 6-9 202
#33 Watson 6-7 172
#24 Bradford 5-10 156

TOP SUBS
#34 Brooks 6-3 190
#42 Turner 6-3 187
#21 Jones 5-8 130
#22 Warner 5-10 175

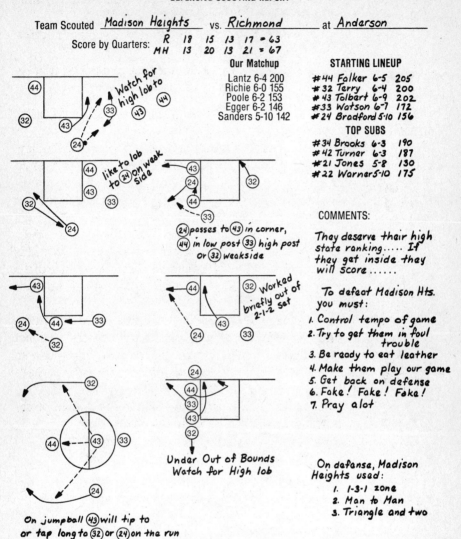

Watch for high lob to

like to lob to (24) on weak side

(24) passes to (43) in corner, (44) in low post (33) high post or (32) weakside

Worked briefly out of 2-1-2 set

Under Out of Bounds Watch for High lob

On jumpball (43) will tip to or tap long to (32) or (24) on the run

COMMENTS:

They deserve their high state ranking..... If they get inside they will score......

To defeat Madison Hts. you must:
1. Control tempo of game
2. Try to get them in foul trouble
3. Be ready to eat leather
4. Make them play our game
5. Get back on defense
6. Fake! Fake! Fake!
7. Pray a lot

On defense, Madison Heights used:
1. 1-3-1 zone
2. Man to Man
3. Triangle and two

Defensive Scouting Report

Diagram 10-22

1. Do they cue patterns with hand signals, voice, etc.? *No*

2. Which side of court do they prefer to start offense? *Either*

3. Will offense change against different defenses? *No*

4. Are they good ball handlers? *Yes*

5. Can they stand pressure? *Yes*

6. Do they fast break? *All the time*

7. Will they as a team take much time to get off a shot? *No*

8. Who are their quickest players? *24, 44*

9. Who are their best and most dangerous players? *44, 43, 33*

10. Best rebounders? *44, 43*
11. Would the Man/Zone bother them?
    Yes it did in prior meetings

12. Offensive pace: Deliberate   (Quick shooting)

13. Do they prefer the inside or will they fire from outside? *Inside*

14. What are their offensive strengths and weaknesses?
    Inside game tough (33) tough outside
    They become frustrated when not hitting!

15. Besides committing suicide, what would you do to defeat them?
    See first page of scouting report

16. Additional comments:

Diagram 10-22 (continued)

Index

Index